MouthSounds

How to whistle, pop, boing, and honk for all occasions . . . and then some.

MouthSounds

How to whistle, pop, boing, and honk for all occasions ... and then some.

Fred Newman

WORKMAN PUBLISHING • NEW YORK

Library of Congress Cataloging in Publication Data is available.

Cover design: Paul Gamarello
Interior design: Kristen Ekeland
Cover photo: Anthony Loew
Interior photos: Chris Carroll
Interior illustrations: Matt Fox
Photo of didgeridoo, page 129, appears courtesy of L.A. Outback.

Workman books are available at special discounts when purchased in bulk
for premiums and sales promotions as well as for fund-raising or educational
use. Special editions or book excerpts can also be created to specification.
For details, contract the Special Sales Director at the address below.

Workman Publishing Company, Inc.
708 Broadway
New York, NY 10003-9555
www.workman.com

Printed in the United States of America
First printing November 2004
10 9 8 7 6 5 4 3 2 1

DEDICATION

This book is dedicated to Lila and Gil John, my daughter and son, and my wife, Katy—all part of what may be the loudest family in the world. We thank our lucky stars that it's physically impossible for us to live next door to ourselves.

This book, too, is dedicated to the sound makers and storytellers I grew up among in Georgia, gentle folk who spun tales with voices and sounds, as naturally as they breathed.

And, lastly, this book is dedicated to those overly enthusiastic little guys—the class clowns and the office cutups—those unsung heroes who, in addition to shooting paper clips and photocopying their faces, rescue us from what might otherwise be lackluster afternoons. I think that covers it.

ACKNOWLEDGMENTS

I would like to thank those people who helped so much in advising, designing, and generally guiding this book to reality (with the thought that, if I include their names, they'll probably buy the book); those who put their self-esteem on the line by allowing us to include their faces (and their belongings for props): Katherine Adzima, David Allender, Suzie Bolotin, Eric Brown, Rozelle Cabon, Anthony Cacioppo, Chris Carroll, Nick Caruso, Anne Cherry, Aaron Clendening, Nicki Clendening, Sharif Corinaldi, Danielle Costa, Sharon Crawford, Kevin Davidson, Beth Demko, Beth Doty, Matt Dunn, Rudy Duran, Jarrod Dyer, Sarah Edmond, Janine Fraser, Nicole Fulmer, Antonia Fusco, Michael Fusco, Philip Gerace, Chloe Godwin, Joe Goldschein, Ellice Goldstein, Shi-Ree Gonzalez, Frank Greeley, Andrew Guertin, Micah Hales, Emilia Hernandez, Margot Herrera, Dan Hertzberg, Kim Hicks, Luke Janka, Tim Jones, Mari Kraske, Cory Leahy, Kevin Leahy, Chris Lee, Molly Macdonald, Melody Meyer, Joni Miller, Deyanisa Moronta, Catherine Newell-Hanson, Lila Newman, Megan Nicolay, Kathy Nunnink, Andra Olenik, Amy Paul, Dove Pedlosky, Anthony Pedone, Barbara Rodriguez, Richard Rosen, Robyn Schwartz, Tod Seelie, Yanfei Shen, Beth Svinarich, Pam Thompson, Lily Tilton, Kate Tyler, Robert Vargas, Howard Warren, Walter Weintz, Melissa White, and Doug Wolff.

I would also like to thank the following: Cliff Hahn and his two ears; the ever-generous Garrison Keillor and those well-above-average folks at *A Prairie Home Companion* who sonically challenge me and graciously share their shows with me, with a special thanks to Sam Hudson; my gentle guide and colleague Faith Hamlin; and those wondrous folks at Workman, who long ago learned to catch a whiff of vision and spin it into something others could see and hold, particularly, Peter and Carolan Workman; the design team, Paul Gamarello, Kristen Ekeland, Patrick Borelli, Miyoung Lee, Lisa Hollander, and Gary Robbins; in type, Barbara Peragine, Jarrod Dyer, and Anne Lamb; in production, Wayne Kirn, Katherine Adzima, Elizabeth Gaynor, Marta Jaremko, and Justin Nisbet; in publicity, Mari Kraske and Kim Hicks; photographers Chris Carroll and Tony Loew; and, most notably, big cheese editor Suzie Bolotin, for her enthusiasm, good humor, and deft sense of balance. And finally, a huge, special thanks to Megan Nicolay, my editor and comrade, who did the heavy lifting—sifting and sorting, elbowing and inspiring throughout. Wuh-tchiii! Thanks for the sound of the finger whip.

CONTENTS

CHAPTER 8: **RUDE NOISES**

CHAPTER 9: **CREATING VOICES** 189

CHAPTER 10: **SOUND STORIES** 219

THE MOUTHSOUNDS CD

Your *MouthSounds* enhanced CD is the action-packed, three-dimensional sound companion to the book. As an audio CD, it demonstrates every sound, voice, and story in the book (including some special audio extras like clips from Garrison Keillor's *A Prairie Home Companion*), along with video clips, playable on your computer. All the sounds on the CD are mouth-made and acoustic—served up piping hot, with absolutely no electronic processing—delivered unplugged and in your face as if the author were sitting directly in front of you.

IT'S JUST THIS EASY . . .

For your ears:
Use the enhanced CD as a guide. As you work through the book, listen to each sound and always try the sound out loud. Just pop your *MouthSounds* CD in any audio player and hit play. Because the CD was recorded in three-dimensional, binaural sound (see below), it works particularly well when you're wearing headphones, or when it's played through stereo computer speakers placed hard left and right—the sounds will seem to float around your head.

Each sound in the book is marked with its CD track number, like this: ⊙ 17

For your eyes:
When you see the following icon, you will know there is a corresponding piece on the enhanced CD for you to watch:

Place the CD in the CD-ROM player of any relatively new computer, follow the menu, and you can view any of the demonstrations and video clips.

WHAT'S BINAURAL SOUND?

Binaural sound is a kind of ultra-realistic, three-dimensional stereo sound. It is recorded with microphones placed *in the ears* of a dummy head. That's right, just inside the ears of a human-size, plastic dummy head having realistic ears and hair. Why? Because it most closely duplicates the way you would actually hear the sound had you been there when it was recorded. The artificial head is a stand-in for *your* head during the recording.

Your ears act as filters—sounds coming at you from the back sound differently than those sounds coming at you from the side or front. Your brain, using this subtle sound shading, along with the tiny timing differences between your left and right ears, instantly deciphers and locates the sound. You hear the sound of footsteps, say, to the left, behind you.

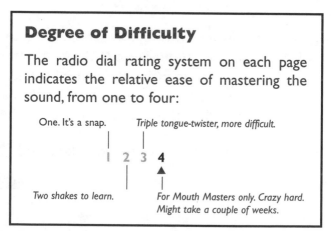

Degree of Difficulty

The radio dial rating system on each page indicates the relative ease of mastering the sound, from one to four:

One. It's a snap.   *Triple tongue-twister, more difficult.*

1 2 3 **4**
         ▲

Two shakes to learn.   *For Mouth Masters only. Crazy hard. Might take a couple of weeks.*

PLEASE NOTE . . . YOUR VOLUME CONTROL

It's important that you set your volume level appropriately for the audio portion of the CD, partly for ear safety, but mostly for 3-D clarity. Set your listening levels on Track 1, so that something like the fly that buzzes around your head sounds very natural to you. It should sound very present, inches away from your ears (not scary-loud or too soft and distant).

INTRODUCTION

(DON'T FLIP PAST THIS. IT AIN'T JUST FLUFFY STUFF.)

"My favorite question is not *how* you make some whistle or honk or bark, but . . . *why*?"

Civilizations come and go. The swish of arrows is replaced by the crack of rifles. Gallops give way to engine whirrs. The clink of chalices becomes the crunch of Dixie cups. We know our society by the sounds that pour forth.

Sounds provide the cues by which we pace our lives. We begin the day with the zing of the alarm clock. The creak of the opening door tells us the bathroom is free. The teakettle whistles. The telephone rings. The microwave dings. The cat meows at the door.

The subtleties of sounds provide clues that communicate and connect us to the world we live in. But these days so many sounds spew forth that we are overwhelmed. The tide of normal daily sound has risen extraordinarily—most of the sounds we hear in an average day did not even exist a generation before. We now swim in a noisy sonic sea, awash in rumbles and drones, in staccato blips of modern gadgetry and cell-phone chatter. Many of us carry around our own spheres of personal audio sound—satellited, downloaded, or mp3'd, shaped and sculpted for us. We are numbed, so pulled back, that we could live a lifetime without once pausing to appreciate the croak of a toad, the whisper of wind, or the crackle of cellophane.

MouthSounds is a book that is as much about listening as it is about imitating sounds, because to imitate, we must first listen—*really* listen. We must let the sound enter us and become a part of us, like a language. We can actually learn to speak sound.

And we are uniquely prepared. No other creature on earth, no instrument ever devised, has the creative ability to manipulate sounds as does the human voice. We talk, yell, whisper, laugh, sing, and make all manner of sounds with extraordinary range and natural ease. Yet most of us barely even notice the sound of our own voice.

By attempting to imitate sounds around us, we learn to listen to that voice. We limber it up and shake it out. We add youthfulness and flexibility. We brush past inhibitions. We extend our vocabulary into new realms of acoustic color. We learn to better use our voice to communicate and entertain, astound and amuse. And we can garnish a story or a conversation with sound effects sure to widen eyes and raise eyebrows.

MouthSounds speaks to the whistles, pops, boings, and honks that lie within each of us.

AN EXCURSION INTO THE MOUTH

THE RAND MCNALLY OF THE ORAL CAVITY

The human voice mechanism is an amazing thoroughfare. From the back roads of the lungs, air passes over the vocal folds, generating sound vibrations. These vibrations travel up the four-lane highway of the throat into the echoing valleys of the mouth and nose, where the peculiarity of the scenery (such as post-nasal drip) adds color, variety, and distinctive richness to the sound.

The sound vibrations then motor over the tongue and through the teeth and lips, where they are drawn out and clipped into sounds or words. They speed out of the mouth and into the ears of listeners. It is a quick trip, taking only fractions of a second to accomplish—easily our most reliable route for sending messages to others.

The vocal mechanism is really an instrument that involves the coordinated use of several separate structures of the body: the lungs, which act as the power source; the vocal folds, which generate the sound vibration; and the throat, nose, and mouth, which act as resonators and amplifiers of the sound.

The Lungs

The lungs, for our purposes, are like a pair of kitchen trash bags suspended in the chest cavity. They just hang there. They have no ability to move or inflate themselves, but, as we breathe, they are filled with air by the contraction and relaxation of our chest muscles, in particular the diaphragm. The lungs provide the air pressure necessary to make the vocal folds vibrate.

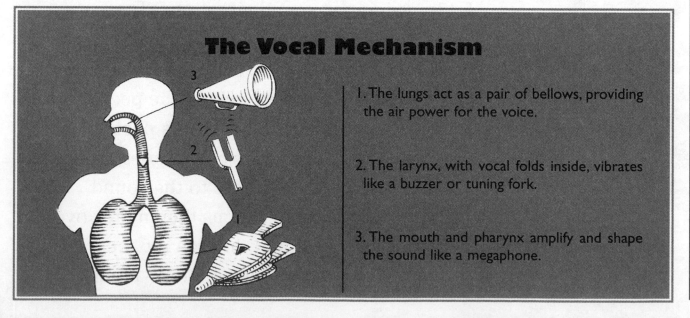

The Vocal Mechanism

1. The lungs act as a pair of bellows, providing the air power for the voice.

2. The larynx, with vocal folds inside, vibrates like a buzzer or tuning fork.

3. The mouth and pharynx amplify and shape the sound like a megaphone.

The Inhale

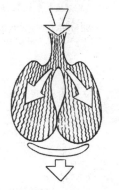

The diaphragm is contracted and lowered, enlarging the chest cavity and drawing in air.

The Exhale

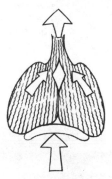

The diaphragm is relaxed, shrinking the chest cavity and pressing out air from our lungs.

The Diaphragm

The diaphragm is the single most important muscle in breathing. It is a powerful dome-shaped sheet of muscle that separates the chest cavity from the abdominal cavity. Inhalation takes place when we contract, flatten, and lower the diaphragm, enlarging the chest cavity and thereby pulling air into our lungs. To exhale, we simply relax the diaphragm; it settles back to a dome shape, shrinking the chest cavity, and air is pressed from our lungs. When we speak loudly or sing, we squeeze other abdominal and chest muscles, forcing more rapid and controlled exhalation of air.

The Larynx

The larynx, or what vocal unsophisticates call the "voice box," is the tube-shaped mechanism in the throat that houses and supports the vocal folds. It consists of many delicate muscles and nine cartilages, the most prominent of which forms the hard lump in the throat we call the Adam's apple. Air exhaled from the lungs passes through the larynx between the vocal folds, making them vibrate.

The Vocal Folds

Nearly every birthday party has a beetle-browed, twelve-year-old kid—or some guy from accounting—who blows up a party balloon, stretches out the sides of the neck, and pinches out a particularly penetrating, rubbery squeal (errr-eeeEEEE!). Although we may find their behavior obnoxious, they are merely demonstrating how our vocal folds work.

Vocal folds should not be called "vocal cords," for they are not cordlike at all, but actually two enfoldings (much like the pinched balloon) of the mucous membrane that lines the larynx. They are connected across the vacuum-cleaner hose of the windpipe (or *trachea*, for you know-it-alls) in an elastic, V-shaped configuration. The two vocal folds are fixed together at the front of the throat, with the other end of each fold connected separately to two mobile cartilages at the back of the throat. The cartilages are moved by muscles that pull the vocal folds together, allowing them to vibrate in the stream of air from the lungs.

To whisper, we pull the folds only slightly together, but for full speech or singing, the folds are drawn in completely. Try whispering an "ahh" sound and moving slowly to a full-voiced "ahh." You'll feel the sensation of your larynx moving the vocal folds inward. (Do this in public and watch people stare at you.)

Using a very complex array of muscles in and around the larynx, we change the pitch of our vocal sounds. To sing the familiar "do, re, mi" musical scale, various muscles stretch our vocal folds, making them thinner and tighter. The more we stretch them, the thinner the vocal folds, the faster the vibrations, and the higher the pitch of the tone—just like the party jackass stretching the neck of a party balloon.

The False Vocal Folds

Directly above the vibrating, sound-making vocal folds are two "false vocal folds." The false vocal folds are little flaps used to help protect the lungs from inhaling debris. When the false folds are tightly drawn together, they help us hold our breath. Not a huge deal, you might think. But our lungs would collapse were it not for the fact that we involuntarily hold our breath when we exert ourselves physically. In activities ranging from lifting kids to swinging a golf club, we automatically hold our breath to protect our lungs from collapse. Ever notice that a person over forty grunts as he leans over to pick up the remote control? That's the sound of air slipping past those little flaps—yes, it's the sound of your false vocal folds at work.

Cutaway View of the Vocal Folds

(Looking down our vacuum-cleaner-hose of a windpipe)

Vocal folds relaxed at sides of windpipe for normal breathing

Vocal folds drawn in slightly for a soft whisper

Vocal folds drawn closer together for a loud "stage" whisper

Vocal folds pulled completely together for full vibration or normal speech

Breathing: Good.
Not Breathing: Bad.

Fortunately, breathing is automatic. But there is still some skill involved, and many people breathe incorrectly. Correct breathing is important not only for good health but also for good honking. We often breathe only with our upper chest by raising and lowering the rib cage, but this type of breathing is shallow and inefficient.

Correct breathing involves breathing from the belly, or, more correctly, breathing from the diaphragm. When we sleep, the body naturally breathes this way to conserve energy.

Try this exercise: Get horizontal. (Lie down on the floor.) Place your hand on your stomach and feel your stomach rise and fall from your diaphragm. Now sit up straight and continue breathing slowly from your stomach. This is how you should always breathe.

Good posture and correct breathing actually improve your projection and ability to speak by helping proper breath control. Because many of the sounds included in this book (like honks and horns) require large amounts of air, proper breathing is especially important.

SOUND SHAPING:
THE PHARYNX, MOUTH, AND NOSE

The pharynx is a complex elastic chamber inside your throat, from the back of your mouth down to your vocal folds. The roof of the pharynx is the soft palate, or velum, which acts as the opening and closing doorway to the nasal cavities. The vibrations of your voice, generated in the vocal folds of the larynx, are shaped and strengthened within the pharynx, mouth, and nasal passages, just the way resonant chambers (sound boxes) amplify and add to the fundamental tones of instruments like guitars or violins.

As the pharynx, mouth, and nose cavities vibrate with vocal tones, sound overtones increase, giving the human voice its unique richness and versatility. Relaxing the muscular walls of the pharynx dampens the higher frequencies of the voice and

(continued on page 7) **5**

The Vocal Mechanism

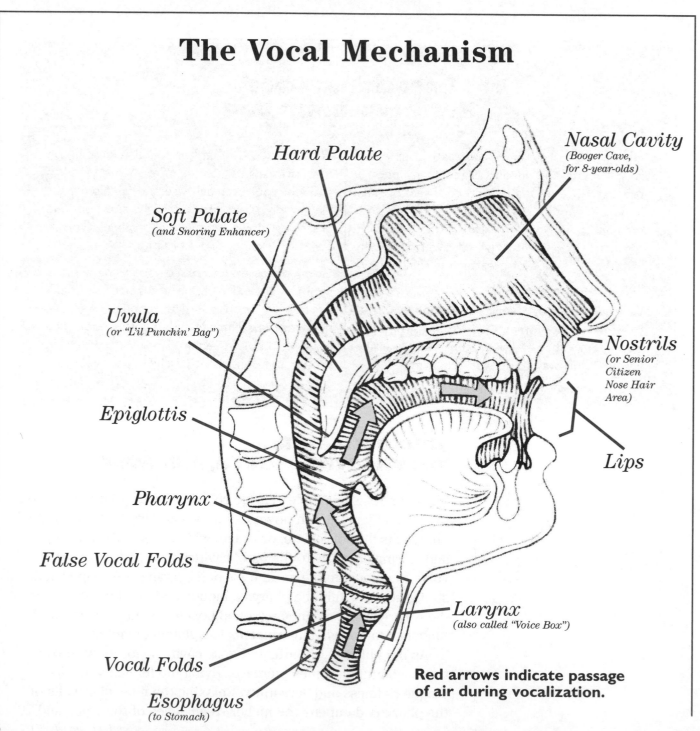

Hard Palate

Nasal Cavity
(Booger Cave,
for 8-year-olds)

Soft Palate
(and Snoring Enhancer)

Uvula
(or "L'il Punchin' Bag")

Nostrils
(or Senior
Citizen
Nose Hair
Area)

Epiglottis

Lips

Pharynx

False Vocal Folds

Larynx
(also called "Voice Box")

Vocal Folds

**Red arrows indicate passage
of air during vocalization.**

Esophagus
(to Stomach)

Helloooo, Big Boy . . .

The soft, low, sexy purr of a female voice used by Madison Avenue to hawk anything from automobiles to panty hose is no accidental advertising ploy. The sexiness of that husky whisper rests squarely in biology: During sexual excitement and lovemaking, the mucous membrane of the larynx undergoes physical changes that cause the voice, particularly the female voice, to become lower and huskier. The soft, low coos of singers and film stars are imitations of this sexual voice. Admired by men and simulated by women, this voice has nearly universal, cross-cultural sexual appeal.

(continued from page 5)

accentuates the lower frequencies, producing a softer, more mellow voice. Hard or taut muscular walls act more like reflectors, usually producing more projection and brighter, sharper tones. Voice training involves this "shaping" of the sound as much as it does hitting notes and finding correct pitch. Trained singers learn to control the muscles to get just the right balance of pleasant, relaxed sound and strong projection.

Words and speech are formed when the pharynx and back of the mouth change size and shape to produce the voiced vowel sounds ("a," "e," "i," "o," "u") and the tongue and lips glide, dampen, and clip tones into consonants (sounds like "buh," "fuh," "wuh," "mmmm," "ti" and "ssss"). Notice these consonants are formed more at the front of the mouth, while "rrrr" and "guh" are formed in the back with the tongue. When these nuances combine with our ever-changing pitch, we create the world's most expressive instrument.

. . . And That Little Punching Bag Back There

No doubt you have noticed the little hangy-down-thingy from the soft palate in the back of your mouth. That thingy is the *uvula*

(Latin for "little grape"), which, although it serves no apparent purpose itself, is really interesting to look at in the mirror. (Most of us agree that it is the perfect punching bag for a plucky cartoon mouse who has just been eaten by a cartoon cat.)

Maybe you've noticed, particularly if you eat Ben and Jerry's ice cream alone in the kitchen, that it is quite possible to hum *and* chew food at the same time. (Note: It's considered rude and potentially life altering at a candlelight dinner for two.) How is humming and chewing possible? Try this: Breathe in and out through your nose, and open your mouth at the same time. Pretend to chew. You can hum, too, if you like. You have raised your soft palate (or velum) and closed off your nasal cavities from your mouth. And guess what? You do this naturally when

Cough It Up

Without the use of our false vocal cords and their ability to coordinate a cough, we would be unable to clear our lungs of unpleasant things such as excess mucus or bean dip that's gone down the wrong tube.

During a cough, we quickly inhale air as the diaphragm descends forcefully. The vocal folds and false vocal folds close tightly. As we tense our abdominal muscles, air pressure builds in our lungs to the point that the folds are suddenly exploded apart, and the unwanted mucus—or lump of bean dip—is expelled.

Coughs are most often a spontaneous bodily reaction to the tickle of unwelcome matter in the lungs, but occasionally we can use the cough to social advantage. A feigned coughing attack allows you an acceptable quick exit from such tedious situations as investment lectures, the ballet, droning church sermons, and high-school productions of *Brigadoon*. A fake coughing attack can part a concert crowd like the Red Sea or get you to the front of a bathroom line at sporting events, especially when ushered by a friend shouting, "Excuse me, 'scuse me. Sick person comin' through." (Coughing suggests psychologically to crowds that throw-up might be involved.)

These lifesaving uses for the cough cannot be overestimated. Indeed, the cough is nothing to be sneezed at.

you gargle or swallow. This talent is important for some of the sounds you'll learn later, too. (See the Ploit Principle, page 24.) And it is of course key for humming and eating ice cream.

Your Friend, the Epiglottis

Your throat multitasks. It holds two distinct pipes: the windpipe (also called the trachea), which goes to your lungs; and the "food pipe," or esophagus, which goes to your stomach. The little leaf-shaped gatekeeper is the *epiglottis*.

The epiglottis is a flap of cartilage, not much bigger than a quarter, located at the base of the tongue, just in front of the entrance to the larynx, or voice box. When it's at rest, the epiglottis is upright and lets air pass through the larynx into the lungs. When you swallow, it works like a lid on the larynx, closing to prevent any Pepsi or Doritos from entering the windpipe. At the end of each swallow, the epiglottis moves up again, the larynx returns to rest, and the flow of air into the windpipe resumes. Sometimes the correct sequence of swallowing gets tangled and the epiglottis doesn't close in time—whammo! Food "goes down the wrong way," and there's that big choking, coughing scene in the restaurant.

In terms of evolution, the epiglottis is a vestigial remnant of a larger cartilage flap once used to seal off the mouth from the nasal passages while chewing. By doing so, our defensive sense of smell would not be interfered with during eating.

Your Brain

Exactly how the brain controls the voice is not completely understood. We do know that, unlike other animals, humans have several centers in the dominant brain hemisphere that aid in vocalization. Usually, at least for right-handed people, these centers are located on the left side of the brain near the temple,

The Vocal Control Center

Broca's Area

Wernicke's Area

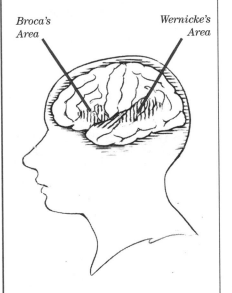

in a part of the brain known as Broca's area. This area controls the muscles of the mouth and throat and coordinates other complex bodily movements (such as breathing) that are essential for speech and singing.

A second center, Wernicke's area—located just behind Broca's area—is responsible for the structure and sense of our language. As we speak, Wernicke's area takes auditory information from our ears as feedback, and informs the speaker about such qualities as pitch, volume, and inflection of the voice.

When we want to say something like "Yo, hold the mustard," Wernicke's area organizes words into a basic grammatical form and then quickly sends signals to Broca's area to coordinate breathing, vocal folds, mouth, throat, and lips so that a quick "Yo!" comes out just in time.

It is interesting that singing, as opposed to speaking, involves separate neural mechanisms that are located deep within primitive areas of the brain that deal with emotional activity. Often, when a stroke causes such brain damage that a person cannot speak, the person is still able to sing with fine articulation, and many severe stutterers can sing without problem.

The complexities of speaking and singing require a great deal of brain space—so much so that there are slight lumps over Broca's and Wernicke's areas, making the left side of the brain larger than the right.

In Your Ear

The human ear responds to sound vibrations that are really minute changes in air pressure repeated in rapid succession. It is so sensitive to waves of sound vibrations that changes in atmospheric pressure of one part in ten billion, if repeated

Earlids

The ear, like the voice, is an astounding instrument. Our hearing has evolved as our most important defense mechanism, giving us the ability to sense predators or enemies in total darkness.

You will note that although we have eyelids that close when we sleep, we have no earlids—sound was always too important to close out.

Deafness is considered by psychologists to be the most profound of sensory losses. If one cannot hear, it is extremely difficult to learn to navigate the world and speak. (Modern teaching techniques for the hearing impaired have helped greatly, however.)

We learn to speak and sing—and make all sorts of vocal sounds—almost exclusively by imitation. We hear first, then try to vocalize the sound, and then, hearing our resultant attempt, adjust our voice and try again. It is said that the best singers, comedians, and storytellers are those who have learned to truly listen, especially to their own voices.

about 3,500 times a second, send audible signals to the brain. In receiving such a sound, the eardrum moves less than one-tenth the diameter of the smallest atom. In fact, if our ears were more sensitive, we would probably be able to hear the motion of air molecules as they vibrate with heat energy.

Humans can distinguish sound vibrations ranging from a low of about 16 vibrations per second (the lowest bass note you can hear) to a high of about 20,000 per second (overtones of violins), with heightened sensitivity to those sounds falling within the range of 1,000 to 4,000 vibrations per second.

TYPES OF VOICES

The adult singing voice is classified according to its range. Each voice has its own peculiarities but, in general, male voices are roughly divided into basses, baritones, and tenors, while female voices are divided into contraltos, mezzo-sopranos, and sopranos.

(See the chart below outlining these categories and the approximate range of each.)

Vocal Range

Pitch is determined by the speed with which the vocal cords vibrate to produce the tone of the voice. Pitch is measured in vibrations or cycles per second or *Hertz* (abbreviated *Hz*), or in thousands of cycles per second, *kilohertz* (*kHz*). The range of the voice is dependent upon the size of the larynx as related to sex, age, and body type, while the exact pitch within a given

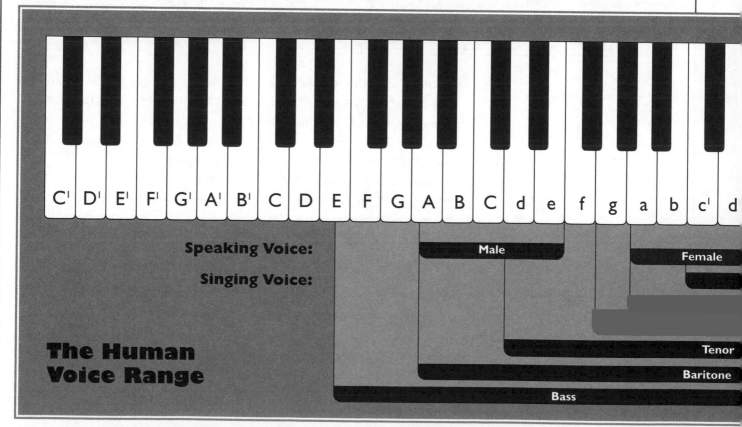

The Human Voice Range

Speaking Voice:

Singing Voice:

C¹ D¹ E¹ F¹ G¹ A¹ B¹ C D E F G A B c d e f g a b c¹ d

Male

Female

Tenor

Baritone

Bass

range is dictated by such variables as tension of the vocal folds and air pressure.

Speaking vs. Singing

Gliding voice inflections combined with sudden changes in volume and pitch give meaning to syllables. Usually the pitch will slide up and down a limited scale of tones—about one octave, three or four notes above and below a middle note. In Western cultures, males tend be more monotonic, while females tend towards a wider range.

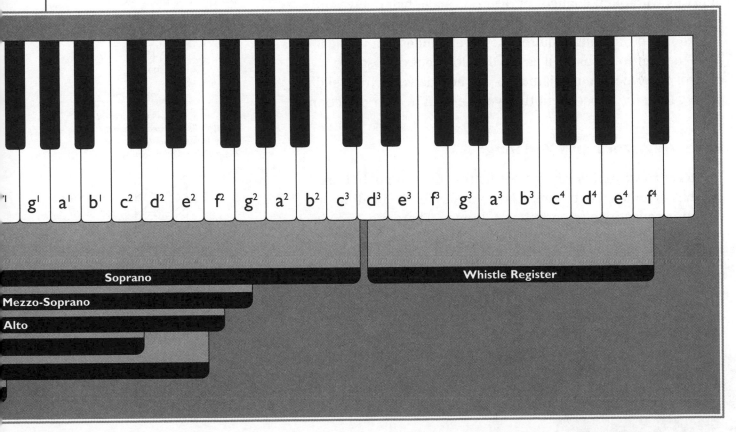

Highs and Lows

The lowest note written for vocal performance is a low D, 73 cycles per second (D$_2$), at the end of Osmin's aria in Mozart's opera *The Abduction from the Seraglio.* The highest note is a high F, almost 1,400 cycles per second (F$_6$), sung by the Queen of Night in *The Magic Flute.* (See chart, pages 12 and 13.)

Singing requires all the skills that speaking does, but demands increased breath capacity and control over longer phrases. Singing usually has a rhythmical melody over precise musical intervals with pitch changes of over one-and-a-half octaves in untrained voices and three or more octaves in trained voices. Unlike speech, singing requires the development of a musical "ear" to hear notes, as well as the development of absolute control over vocal musculature to prevent the voice from sliding off key (and the subsequent throwing of stuff in your direction).

Vocal Registers and Yodeling

The term *vocal register* is not a scientific term at all, but one that has been used over centuries to describe the location of vibrating sensations of certain vocal tones. There are three basic registers: the chest voice, mid-voice, and head voice, reflecting the fact that low notes are felt primarily in the chest, and high notes are felt in the head and nasal areas.

The chest voice may be more scientifically called the *thick voice,* because a cross-section of the vibrating vocal folds shows that the lowest tones are produced by a marked thickening and lengthening of the full vocal folds, forming a richer tone, full of resonant chest vibrations.

THE VOICE
Through Thick and Thin

A front view, cross-section of the vocal folds:

Thick register or chest voice: vocal folds thickened by relaxed muscles for lower notes.

Mid-voice or passaggio register: vocal folds thinned somewhat as voice transitions to thinner head voice. Yodel occurs here.

Thin register or head voice: vocal folds pulled very thin. Mostly edges of vocal folds vibrate.

The mid-voice (called *Passaggio*, or "passing voice") uses some of the fullness of the chest voice; however, the vocal folds are shortened and thinned a bit, so that they do not vibrate in their entirety, but more at their edges. Classical vocal training attempts to smooth this unstable portion of the voice so that the natural "break" (which occurs as the voice suddenly shifts from the thick voice to the thin voice) passes smoothly, becoming virtually undetectable. In direct contrast, many singers around the world, as far flung as the Appenzellers of Switzerland, Saami of Scandinavia, Pygmies of Central Africa, Hawaiians, and cowboys of the western United States, celebrate and enhance this natural vocal break to create elaborate yodeling —styles that vary from slapstick to tearful to ethereal and meditative.

In the head voice, or *thin voice*, high notes are produced by tensing and thinning the vocal folds to create a less "rounded" sound that resonates primarily in the upper throat, mouth, and nose.

Higher still is another register used by the highest of trained sopranos. It is called the *whistle register*, and is called so because the vocal folds are tensed to a razor-sharp edge, allowing a small, elliptical hole to form between them. The vocal folds do not even vibrate. The singer, often referred to as a *coloratura* soprano, literally whistles through this small hole.

A BRIEF HISTORY OF SPEECH

Just when and why man developed the distinctively human characteristic of speech continues to be wrapped in speculation. It is generally thought, however, that in the three billion years of evolutionary cakewalk that has taken us from primordial sludge to Tom Cruise, man's capacity to speak came very late.

(continued on page 17) **15**

Men Singing Like Women

The *falsetto*, or "false voice," is created by relaxing and elongating the vocal folds so that only the edges of the two folds vibrate. It has a softer, more whispery sound and has been used by men for centuries to reach notes above their normal range.

After the passing of the castrati (see the box on page 18), interest in the male falsetto voice waned during the first half of the twentieth century. Use of falsetto singing was limited to English church choirs, novelty vaudeville acts, and what were known as Negro minstrel shows.

In the late 1940s, however, a revival of falsetto occurred among black spiritual song groups. These groups influenced the high harmonies of popular a cappella doo wop singing in the 1950s. In the 1960s, '70s, and '80s, groups such as the Four Seasons and the Beach Boys, along with the likes of Smokey Robinson and the Miracles, the Chi Lites, the O'Jays, the Stylistics, and the Bee Gees made wildly successful use of soft, falsetto harmonies.

Although falsetto technique had been used for years to extend the range of classically trained tenors or countertenors, true falsetto witnessed a revival in orchestral music in 1960 when the role of Oberon in Benjamin Britten's opera *A Midsummer Night's Dream* was sung in falsetto.

With its long if somewhat checkered history, high-voiced male singing still percolates world pop charts with a number of more recent guy groups from Boys II Men to 98° and OutKast to solo artists Michael Jackson and Justin Timberlake. Their tight, falsetto harmonies, combined with rap and rock influences, have created a distinctively lucrative sound.

(continued from page 15)

Sometime around two million years B.C., our ancestor the *Australopithecus* turned from a vegetarian diet to a menu that included meat—possibly as a result of climatic changes. One theory suggests that meat, as a more concentrated protein source, effectively cut by two-thirds the time spent gathering berries and various fruits, and with more free time, man was able to extend himself in creative and social directions. An increasingly complex hunting and food-gathering society resulted, with increased demands for communication.

Imagine, for example, an unarmed, naked man trying to fell a rampaging woolly mammoth. Without the development of weapons—and language to coordinate other naked men—the woolly mammal would have had the upper hand . . . or foot. (In the long process of language development, no doubt, a lot of confused, naked men were flattened.)

During this time, the brain was developing rapidly. With the coming of *Homo erectus* around one million B.C., man's hands were freed for experimentation and tool formation. Manual dexterity grew as the brain developed refinements and areas of specialization. The result was a preference for either left- or right-hand use and the distinctively human characteristic of dominance of one brain hemisphere over the other. By this specialization, brain capacity was increased tremendously, and the areas of speech control became located in a dominant side of the brain (usually the left side for right-handed people).

The vocal mechanism, too, was evolving rapidly, in part because dexterous human hands freed man's oral cavity from the process of direct food-gathering, allowing the development of vocal articulation. The

The Castrati: Giving 'em Up for the High Notes

Few realize that the high-voiced harmonies of doo wop, in groups like the Beach Boys trace their origins back nearly 2,000 years to the Roman era. To achieve such falsetto, the Romans castrated gifted young male singers. As one can imagine, this put a stop to the natural maturation of their voices, producing singers known as *soprani falsetti*. These singers enjoyed privileged positions among the Roman elite for many years, but with the crumbling of the Roman empire, they quickly disappeared.

In the early sixteenth century, the Renaissance witnessed a rekindling of interest in Greek and Roman culture. Since women were not allowed to sing in choirs, youths were again recruited for *soprani falsetti* or *castrati*, as they were called in the Middle Ages. By the mid-sixteenth century, the castrati were a part of religious celebrations in Spain, and in 1562, Father Soto, a well-known Spanish castrato, drew official church recognition of the castrati upon his admission to the Sistine Chapel choir.

The castrati soon dominated the art of singing. For almost two hundred years, it was a virtual tradition among noted families to have a family member in a leading church choir, and castration was frequently used to uphold this tradition.

By the end of the 1800s, castration for the sake of music was looked upon as a bit extreme, and the castrati were replaced by young male singers and falsettists. Alessandro Moreschi, the last castrato (and the only one to have ever been recorded), retired in 1913 and died in 1922.

vocal folds, originally protective flaps for the windpipe, began to be used to produce primitive sounds for communication. The larynx, containing the vocal folds, descended, and the upper throat (the pharynx) became wider, thus allowing more resonant vocal possibilities and the capacity for producing a range of consistent vowel sounds.

All these advances occurred quite quickly in terms of evolution, with each development being intimately linked to others. Man's manual experimentation contributed to his brain development, which, in turn, aided speech development. At the same time, the invention of spoken words meant an imposition of mental order on the world. This allowed man to *think* more effectively, thus enhancing his intellectual facilities.

Recent theories suggest that the evolution of human speech made great leaps forward about seventy thousand years ago, during the era of the fourth ice age.

From that point on, the social evolution of man exploded. Population began to increase, spurred by the cultural sophistication that arose from language and speech development. Primitive *Homo sapiens* (humans) inhabited the world. Writing was invented. Three thousand languages developed. And modern humans stepped forth to claim dominance over the world.

What's the Buzz?

We are deeply affected by the sounds and rhythms of the sonic environment around us, and can even begin to imitate those patterns. For instance, wherever you go in the world, in every language, the accents of people living in urban city centers are faster, more abrupt, and more clipped than the accents of people living in rural country settings.

Another example, and an interesting fact to pull out at a cocktail party: When asked, after a short period of silence, to hum a note that seems to rise "from their center," people in North America tend to hum the note B-natural. Can you imagine why? Here's a little clue: Europeans tend to hum an A-flat. Any ideas?

Give up? The answer is this: North America has a 60-cycle electrical current, and Europe has a 50-cycle current. In each place, the resonant frequency of all electrical devices—motors, lights, transformers, audio systems, and the like—is the vibration of electrical current and its harmonics. In North America, 60 cycles a second most closely corresponds to the frequency of a B. In Europe, 50 cycles corresponds closely with an A-flat. (Coincidentally, Earl Scruggs, master 5-string banjo picker, grew up tuning the B-string of his banjo to the hum of a fluorescent lamp.)

Electricity literally provides the base note of our modern culture. It is inside us. It is a part of us.

PRINCIPLES OF MOUTHSOUNDS

Mouthsounds are really oral acrobatics, a kind of vocal tai chi. No less than yoga or playing an instrument, they demand the delicate orchestration of muscles—almost 60 muscles, in fact, just to sing the notes do, re, mi. They require patience—mostly with yourself, as you develop muscle coordination and an ear; first to *hear* the sounds, then to *try* the sounds, and, finally, to *fine-tune* the many, completely new sounds and voices that will be flowing out of you. Sound making, like life, requires a playful, fearless spirit: you have to be willing to look and sound like a moron and act in exactly the manner teachers told you not to. And, you must be able to weather the eye rolls and stares of those who cannot fathom why.

For the Zen of MouthSounds, simply follow the path of The 7 Steps, outlined here:

On Becoming a Master: The 7 Steps

Step 1 Listen to the *MouthSounds* Enhanced Audio CD. The CD (enhanced with demo video clips and sound stories when placed in a computer) enables you to hear each of the sounds and voices described in the book, and it gives you an idea of the range of vocal possibilities.

Step 2 Read the first two chapters. They provide a basic understanding of the voice, several basic sounds, and some interesting tidbits for you to drop into casual conversation and cocktail chatter.

Step 3 Always try the sounds and voices out loud. You can flip randomly through the book or try one that catches your ear on the CD. For your own sake, do this in a secluded spot or in the company of stoners and/or understanding friends—not on a cross-town bus.

Step 4 Work up the nerve to try out a few sounds with others, in a lull in conversation over the water cooler, or to accent a point at dinner. You will be surprised how the sounds can lighten up a business presentation, book report, or political discussion. Try injecting a few voices into a story or joke or when ordering at a Wendy's drive-thru. Or, try out one of the sound stories on a willing (if overly sleepy) child.

Step 5 Use the book and CD as party entertainment. It's great fun to hear others attempt the sounds. And, more importantly, you increase your own self-esteem by making others look foolish.

Step 6 Log on to *www.mouthsounds.info* to check for any updates, new sounds, tips and techniques, or answers to frequently asked questions.

Step 7 Begin listening to sounds around you, pulling them into your new and rapidly expanding repertoire. It is all about listening and drawing sounds into your being, making them become a part of you. With each new sound or voice you master, you develop increased vocal flexibility, improving your ability to master even more. Don't be discouraged if you can't produce sounds immediately. Persevere. With a little bit of effort, you will soon be able to dazzle, delight, and yes, even stupefy your fellow life travelers—or, failing that, bug the crap out of them.

THE FALSETTO

True falsetto is the high-pitched, slightly breathy voice that can be affected by most people. Falsetto is produced by allowing only a part of the vocal folds to vibrate—the vocal folds are thinned in such a way that vibrations occur mostly on the inner edges of the folds. In male falsetto, the thin vibrating portion of the vocal folds closely approximates the size of the female vocal folds, thus making the high falsetto of a male sound much like a slightly whispery female voice. Many of the sounds in *MouthSounds* will require the use of this voice in males or a similar high-pitched voice in females, so get practicing!

INSTRUCTIONS

You may already be able to produce a falsetto voice easily, but if you cannot, do the following:
1. In a normal tone, let the pitch of your voice glide upward from low notes to high notes, *without increasing the volume.* (If you get louder as you glide to the higher notes, you will stay in the "chest voice" and not trigger your falsetto.)
2. Practice talking and singing with the falsetto voice. At some point for males, and most females, your voice will "break" as it gets higher. You will hear a sudden distinct change in the quality of your voice as the falsetto thinning of the vocal fold vibration occurs. This break, by the way, is the basic principle of yodeling.

Many cartoon and puppet voices, such as *Sesame Street's* Ernie and Muppets' Kermit the Frog and Miss Piggy are created by using the falsetto (see Chapter 9, "Creating Voices").

For falsetto, only the thin edge of the vocal folds vibrates.

THE PLOIT

The Ploit, a hollow thump of a sound, illustrates the basic principle of resonance.

Resonance

Besides the vocal folds, the most important tool in your noisemaking toolbox is resonance. When you whistle, click, or pop, you do not use your vocal folds or voice at all. It is possible to use your lips or tongue or even your hands to cause vibrations that are then molded into a sound by the shape of your mouth and throat.

INSTRUCTIONS

1. Imagine that you are holding water in your mouth. Breathe normally *through your nose*. This will close off the back of your opened mouth, making it like a hollow cup.

Back of tongue arched up to soft palette to close off mouth.

2. Draw your tongue to the back of your open mouth, as if you were holding even more water in your mouth, and shape your mouth and lips as if you were going to sing a very low "oh." This will allow your cheek to become drumlike.

3. With the pad of your finger, tap or thump the hollow of your cheek as if it were a little drum. (Be sure you are breathing through your nose.) Experiment until you get a clean, resonant thump sound. Congratulations— this is your Ploit.

Gently tap hollow of cheek with finger pad.

4. By pushing your tongue forward—as if you were slowly pushing water out of your mouth—you can raise the pitch of your Ploit to produce musical tones. Practice until you can lilt your way through such favorites as "Yankee Doodle" or "Home on the Range."

Mastering the Ploit principle will serve you well—it forms the basis of many mouth sounds.

THE PALATE GRIND

The Palate Grind is a basic MouthSound technique that forms the foundation of such diverse sounds as hand saws, trains, coffee grinders, and drum rolls. It is the sound many children use to imitate guns and explosions. Like the Ploit, it is a sound technique that does not use your voice.

INSTRUCTIONS

1. Make a "guh" sound, with the hard sound of the "g" in the word *go*. Feel where the back of your tongue touches the roof of your mouth. Now repeat this, arching the back of your tongue upward to touch the top, back of your mouth known as the soft palate.

Exhale, with back of tongue arched up to roof of mouth, as if making a "guh" sound.

2. Exhale so that the back of your tongue and the soft palate vibrate with a gravelly, grinding sound. Be sure to listen to the CD.

3. By moving the arched tongue to different points on the soft palate, varying the air pressure and changing the shape of your mouth and lips, you can produce different grinding tones and sounds.

THE GLOTTAL FRY

Scientists in the field of vocal production, or laryngologists (now, there's a mouthful), invented the term "glottal fry" years ago to describe a particular series of clicking sounds created in the glottis—the opening between the vocal folds in the upper larynx. Although the Glottal Fry does not sound exactly like frying an egg over easy, it's close enough that we can forgive the burst of poetic license. It is a fine sound, in any case, that should become a basic effect in your vocal gadget bag. If you are unsure what you should be hearing, listen to the CD.

INSTRUCTIONS

1. Relax. Sit back in your favorite easy chair. Kick off your shoes. (Notice how odd your little toe looks.)

2. Take in a big breath of air and hold it.

3. Shape your mouth and throat as if you are about to say "aaah."

4. Very slowly, increase the pressure of the air in your chest by pushing from your diaphragm until the air begins to seep out through your vocal folds. (Too much force and you will say "aaah," too little and you will hear an airy whisper.) When you reach vocalization, ease off until you hear a controlled series of low, clipping or little popping sounds. You are officially frying your glottis in the short-order diner of your throat.

USES

While glottal-frying, practice opening your throat and mouth wide to increase resonance and volume. Change the shape of your mouth from an "aah" sound to an "eee" and you'll hear a change in tone. Try reversing this sequence, moving slowly from an "eee" to an "aah," and you'll hear the creaking of a castle door in a low-budget horror movie. Glide upward in pitch, and you have your basic back door opening.

Continuing to glottal fry, shape your mouth as if you were saying an exaggerated "wow." You should be able to click out the "wow" sound as the resonance changes. With practice, you can use the Glottal Fry to talk like a slow, unearthly computer voice. Or, slowed way down to a series of sparse clicks, it becomes a Geiger counter or cosmic ray detector.

THE INHALED FRY

The Inhaled Fry has a much more resonant tone than the regular Glottal Fry because, as you inhale air, it resonates more deeply in your chest.

INSTRUCTIONS

1. Close your vocal folds. To feel how to do this, pretend to hiccup—suddenly inhale a bit of air, and stop it with a "hic." You have closed your vocal folds.

2. With your vocal folds closed, inhale air, slowly increasing force until suddenly you will hear a deep, vocal-frying sound as you inhale. Yep, it is an odd sensation.

3. Open your throat wide, as if to sing the lowest note you can. To increase resonance, form your mouth as if you were making an "o" sound. This configuration will give your Inhaled Fry its deepest, fullest, and loudest sound. It may be a deep growl or an unnatural voice. Practice articulating words in this full voice, while inhaling. You will sound very much like a Hollywood version of an interstellar alien. (See Robot Voice, page 215.)

Hic, Hic . . . The Hiccup

The hiccup is God's little joke on higher vertebrates. The notorious hiccup (or "hiccough" in tonier circles) plagues not only mankind, but all mammals from time to time. The hiccup knows no social boundaries, striking rich and poor alike without warning, reducing all in its grip to a mass of "hics" and apologies. We are particularly vulnerable to a hiccup attack during any suitably inconvenient time, such as a funeral prayer service, dinner with the boss, or just as the police officer leans into your car requesting "License and registration, please."

No one knows exactly what causes hiccups, but they begin with the sudden involuntary contraction of the diaphragm (see diagram, page 3). This results in the sudden, forced inhalation of air and the familiar snaplike closing of the glottis. Hic.

The cures are numerous and equally ineffective. The simplest solution is breathing slowly and deeply into a paper bag until you see stars. The most inventive, perhaps, is to lean over and drink water out of the far lip of a glass. It is messy . . . hic . . . awkward, and potentially hazardous to your health, but grandmothers . . . hic . . . swear by it. Aaah. Hic . . . damn.

CHAPTER 3

POPS, CLICKS, HORNS, HONKS

Pops, clicks, snaps, bangs, horns, and honks make our mechanized world go 'round. Clicks, snaps, and bangs are the by-products of bridled energy, harnessed by man to build, move, take apart, and put together. Horns and honks, on the other hand, are the signals of modern society, meant to prod, poke, provoke, and cajole us into action. Pops? They accent, surprise. They're just for fun. This chapter deals with sounds that continually carom through our lives.

CHAMPAGNE POP

The Champagne Pop is the classic MouthSound, quick and to the point. Historically, it has been used by enterprising adolescents to disrupt more study halls than any other single sound—with the possible exception of the Bronx Cheer.

INSTRUCTIONS

1. As with the Ploit, breathe through your nose to close off the back of your mouth. Insert your index finger into your mouth. (If, at this point, you taste something funny, make a mental note to wash your hands.)

2. Seal your lips around the first knuckle of your finger. Still breathing through your nose, puff out your cheeks.

Pops

Pops come in many shapes and sizes. Some are so faint only mothers can hear them. Others are deafening. Bottles pop, machines pop, even animals pop (remember the weasel?). But in every case, a pop is a clear signal something is happening—or is just about to.

3. Quickly pry your finger out of your mouth so that the tip of the finger snaps the corner—*POP!* It may take a bit of practice, but you will find you can vary the tone and loudness of the pop by varying air pressure, and the angle and speed of your finger.

THE POP 'N' POUR

Combine the Champagne Pop and the Ploit to make the sound of opening a bottle and pouring out its contents. The "pop" is immediately followed by a quick series of Ploits, starting with low tones and rising (as the "bottle" empties). Turn ordinary water into festive bubbly—sonically speaking, of course.

Place the tip of your finger between your lips and puff out your cheeks.

TONGUE FLOP

Ah, the Tongue Flop (aka the Horse Clip-Clop)—one of those MouthSounds that most of us have made at one time or another. It is a simple sound that requires little vocal technology.

INSTRUCTIONS

1. Place your tongue on the roof of your mouth.
2. Tense your tongue a little and pull it away from the roof of your mouth as you drop the jaw to create a slight vacuum.
3. Continue pulling the tongue away and dropping your jaw a bit. Your tongue should flop down on the floor of your mouth with a resonant "plop."

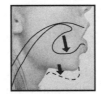

The jaw descends, pulling the tongue off the roof of the mouth.

USES

The Tongue Flop is absolutely grand for one thing: simulating a horse walking down a cobbled street. Clip-clop. Clip-clop. Clip-clop. As you do Tongue Flops, shape your mouth as if you are saying a long "o" (as in goat), alternating with a short "i" (as in pig), and you will hear the clip-clop of horse hooves.

You can also hum while doing the Tongue Flop for horse-riding renditions of "Happy Trails to You," "Red River Valley," or "Surrey with the Fringe on Top" to name a few. Try jingling your car keys, clip-clopping, and humming that Christmas favorite "Sleigh Ride," for a sense-around experience.

With a bit of practice, you can change the shape of your mouth to enable you to tongue flop a musical scale. Try tongue flopping "Yankee Doodle" or "On Top of Old Smokey." Teach several friends to tongue flop "Happy Birthday" and then use a tongue-flopping chorus to serenade a friend with birthday wishes. It will bring tears to their eyes . . . or not.

THE SLAP POP

The Slap Pop is a dynamic way to make a point or cap off an insightful comment. It is made in the same manner as the Ploit (page 24), only you don't gently tap your cheek—you slap your lips. It is a startlingly loud pop that is sure to surprise anyone.

INSTRUCTIONS

1. While breathing through your nose (which causes your mouth to be closed off from your throat), shape your mouth as if you were saying a deep "oh."

2. Do not tense your lips. Keep them loose and O-shaped, with a slight pucker. Take one hand, with fingers together, and lightly slap your lips.

3. Experiment slapping softer and then harder, using different lip tension and mouth shapes.

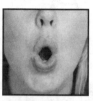

Loose, O-shaped lips. Breathe through your nose.

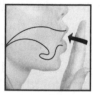

Flat fingers strike slightly puckered lips.

USES

Enter into a discussion or, better still, an outright argument with someone. When you have had your say, lean forward and slap pop in his face. To your opponent, it's a door-slam, telephone-hang-up, toe-stomping, tire-squealing "That's all, folks!"

THE SUCTION POP

The Suction Pop, if executed by a trained sound professional or, failing that, your average eighth-grader, can be one of the loudest of all mouth sounds. It is a hollow konk of a sound that could stun a cat at close range, but if executed gently, can be quite musical, sounding much like tuned, wooden percussion known as temple blocks.

INSTRUCTIONS

1. Place your tongue lightly against the back of your upper teeth, allowing the front edge to seal against the roof of your mouth.
2. Stiffen and tense the tongue, pulling it down a bit, away from the roof of the mouth to create a vacuum against it.
3. Increase the pressure of the vacuum, as your stiffened tongue is drawn down and back away from the top of your mouth. Suddenly, the suction will break with a sharp pop. With a little practice, you can greatly increase the volume and wondrously hollow tone of the pop. (Tip: To "round" the tone, as you increase the suction on the roof of your mouth, shape your mouth as if making an O sound.)

USES

This is a great, general-purpose sound effect for a relatively small object striking something hard and dense (and maybe a little hollow) like: the conk of golf ball off the noggin, the donk of a kick in the shin, or the plonk of a baseball off a bat. You can shape your mouth in different ways to change the tone and pitch of the "pop"—the more you pull the sound back into your mouth and form an O shape with your lips, the more hollow the hit. Even more impressive, try playing melodies and simple songs. Form a duet or a "Suction Pop Choir." "Ode to Joy" in Suction Pops? Beethoven never sounded so fresh.

PING-PONG POPS

Ping-Pong Pops are just that—pops that simulate a hard fought game of Ping-Pong. For all who have hung around YMCAs or basement rec rooms, Ping-Ping Pops are a must.

INSTRUCTIONS

1. Place your tongue tip midway back on the roof of your mouth and seal it lightly against the sides of the roof.

2. Tense the tongue, pulling it away from the roof of the mouth to create a slight vacuum against the roof.

3. Continue tensing the tongue and drop your jaw slightly until you break the vacuum and create a little clicklike "pop." This is the basis for the Ping-Pong Pop.

4. To get the "ping" and the "pong" sounds, alter the shape of your mouth to change the resonance: The "ping" will be the normal pop you made from steps 1 to 3. For the "pong," hold your mouth as if you were pronouncing a long "o" sound.

5. Alternate the "ping" sound with the more hollow "pong" sound.

Timing and rhythm are as important in the imitation as they are in the game itself. Actually, the "pong" sound always precedes the "ping" (think of the paddle as the "pong"; the hard table is the more clicklike "ping"). Make a quick "pong, ping," pause, and then another "pong, ping." Vary the rhythm as demonstrated on the CD

A sharp click of the tongue forms "ping."

More resonant O-shaped mouth forms "pong."

and occasionally let the ball dribble away on the floor.

USES

If you work at it, this can be a very realistic imitation. Walk up to an ordinary table or desk, holding your invisible paddle, and begin playing. Imagine that you are face-to-face with a steely-eyed opponent. Start your imitation and mime play vigorously—even chase the ball across the room as it bounces out of play. If your friends are willing, you can even play doubles.

35

THE TRIPLE CLICK

The Triple Click is an impressive set of three clicks that are produced in rapid succession. The triplets, once mastered, can be used to imitate anything from the sound of Fred Astaire's dazzling tap shoes to the hoof beats of Seabiscuit. Be sure to listen to the CD before trying this.

INSTRUCTIONS

Click One . . .

1. Breathing through your nose, *close your lips* and place the front of your tongue just behind your bottom front teeth. The back of the tongue is arched upward to touch the rear roof of the mouth. A small air pocket should form between your tongue and the front roof of your mouth.

2. Abruptly push your tongue forward to drive out the pocket of air, as if you are spitting out something or saying something like "puht." This will make a little pop or click by blowing the lips slightly apart. (During this move, the portion of the tongue just behind the tip should be pushed forward and up against the upper teeth and roof of your mouth. Practice this until you can make a quick series of little "puht" sounds.

And Click Two . . .

1. After click one, your tongue will be far forward and your lips very slightly apart.

2. Now with a sucking motion, abruptly pull the tongue back, drawing in a just a bit of air, so that the lips snap closed (particularly the bottom lip). This sounds and feels a bit like the way a scolding mother might make little sucking sounds ("tsk, tsk, tsk"). This is click two.

3. Practice pushing and pulling the tongue back and forth to produce clicks one and two, one-two, one-two. Note that the tongue moves only slightly forward and backward to create the clicks.

Now add Click Three . . .

Once you are comfortable with click one and two, add a simple smack by pulling your lips slightly apart with a bit of a suction to make a slight, subtle smack. This is your third click.

This process may seem complex, especially in writing, but listen to the CD and it becomes much simpler to do—with practice. Produce each step in sequence slowly. After click three, start over with click one. Be patient. Triple clicks will probably require a few trial-and-error sessions before they become as natural as click, click, click.

Click 1: *Tongue pushed forward pops lips open.*

Click 2: *Tongue drawn abruptly back clicks lips closed.*

Click 3: *Slight smack of lips leaves mouth open.*

USES

HORSE GALLOPS Use your Triple Click to imitate a galloping horse. Rhythm is important here. Clicks one and two are quick, with emphasis on click three, repeating quickly and smoothly in a "one, two, THREE, one, two, THREE" fashion.

To slow it down to a horse canter, use only click one and two in a four-beat sound. The rhythm should be "one-two, one-two—pause—one-two, one-two—pause—one-two, one-two—pause—."

FRED ASTAIRE TAPS When you can do the Triple Click with ease, you will be able to sound out amazing tap-dance routines with your mouth. Practice by varying the rhythms of the clicks.

Try making your clicks as an accompaniment to records or radio. Better still, hum your favorite tap-dance tunes while you click out the taps.

This hum-and-tap is an impressive effect. Try such standards as "Tea for Two," "Swanee River," or "Moonlight Bay."

Clicks

Clicks are sharp, slight sounds that often go unnoticed. They are the unassuming, auditory workhorses of the mechanical world. They are simple, undemanding noises that give us little clues about big actions around us. A click can be as significant as a phone disconnecting or a lock opening in a horror movie—or as mundane as clipping a toenail.

37

THE FINGER WHIP

The Finger Whip is a turn-around three-point jump shot—an urban snap, a street gesture—used, specifically, to get in someone's face and make a point. It's not so much a sound as it is an effect.

INSTRUCTIONS

1. Take your hand, index finger sticking out, extend it almost at arms length, the *back of your hand* towards the face of the person you want to snap.
2. Now snap your wrist, whip your finger down-

and-up quickly, and make a whip-sound, "whu—tchiii . . . !"

Timing is everything. The sound must be at exactly the moment of the whip gesture. Your whip sound can be hard and aggressive or lazy and more ironic, like you don't give a flyin' . . .

Teeth nearly together, push air out forcefully.

Cocktail Conversation Starter #23: The Speed of Sound

"When do you think humans first broke the sound barrier?" When conversation slows at your next office party or PTA punch 'n' cookies, drop that head-scratcher into the mix.

The answer: No one knows for sure, but most probably during the early Neolithic era or Stone Age. That should cause some puzzlement. When humans first took a strip of animal hide and cracked it like a whip, the sound barrier was broken. How is that possible? The motion created by the quick jerk of the arm is multiplied by a factor of more than thirty times as it travels down the length of a whip. Depending on the temperature and humidity of the air, the tip of the whip can travel at more than 800 miles per hour, roughly the speed of sound. When the whip tip reaches that speed, it actually produces a tiny sonic boom. CRACK!

THE BASIC HONK

There is something in that flat, open quality of a Honk that is downright hilarious. That is why Harpo Marx, cartoon ducks falling on their faces, and now you can use it to great effect.

INSTRUCTIONS

1. Open your mouth and throat wide . . . No. Even wider.
2. With a burst of exhaled air, produce a low-pitched, breathy "hhhaa." (The "a" should be harsh, and sound like the "a" in the word *back*.) The Honk should be aggressive, loud, and full.

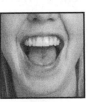

Mouth and throat are opened wide.

USES

Use the Honk to punctuate your conversation. As you produce the Honk, hold your hand in front of you and make a suggestive squeeze.

As you'll see in the following pages, the Basic Honk can be used to initiate a range of honks from a kid's tricycle horn to the blast of a tractor-trailer.

The Big Rig Blast

To sound like an eighteen-wheeler long-haulin' down the expressway, just do the basic honk, but extend it. Make it loud, deep, and long. Add the Doppler effect (see page 134), dropping the pitch as you pass, and you will appear to make your semi (pronounced "sĕm´-ī") roar past a slow coworker.

THE BICYCLE HORN

Imagine the sound of a real, squeeze-bulb bicycle horn. It is actually two sounds: the sharp, deep honk of the squeeze, and the higher-pitched squeak of the release (or "inhale") of the bulb. This is a great example of how you can perform a sound by imitating how it is actually made.

INSTRUCTIONS

1. The bicycle horn is higher pitched that the Basic Honk. Do the Basic Honk, only now with a high falsetto (see page 23) voice. Do this several times, until it is high, nasal, strong and sharp. That is the first part.

2. After you "squeeze the honk," "release the bulb" by inhaling a bit of air back in your open mouth. Just the slightest touch of

falsetto on the inhale completes the bicycle honk beautifully.

USES

This is a great effect for general attention getting or punctuating a conversation—perfect before, say, a PTA or birthday-party announcement. Built in to your Bicycle Horn is a sense of "make-way, coming-thru, pal." Use it for clearing a path through a crowded hallway or sidewalk.

The Bicycle Horn also sounds great over the telephone, just before you say hello—there's no better way to destabilize a mother-in-law or a vacation-deal-pushing telemarketer. A sudden "honk-and-hang up" gets you taken off any call list.

Honks and Horns

The metallic blasts of honks and horns form the backdrop of our cities. The honk is that flat burst of sound that issues forth from the throats of squeeze-bulb bicycle horns and taxi cabs. The horn, on the other hand, is an upper-class version of the honk. (Apparently, one "honks" from the driver's seat of a Volkswagen and "sounds the horn" in a powder-blue Mercedes.) Depending on execution, honks and horns can vary from courtesy beeps to jarring, acoustic assaults.

THE AIR HORN

1 2 3 4 ●
14

The Air Horn is that breathy blast that punctuates time-outs in gymnasium basketball games. It is the "air-horn-in-a-can" that is used by starters (in the distance), at boating events and by jackasses (right behind you) at huge sporting events. Its unsubtle feature is that it's loud as heck—it can blow the toupee off a referee from the top of the bleachers.

INSTRUCTIONS

1. To create a vocal Air Horn, do the Basic Horn, but in a loud, high falsetto. The distinctive sound of an Air Horn comes from an intense stream of air that is squeezed on and choked off, and you need to imitate that with your throat.

2. The high, flat, nasal pitch should swoop down suddenly with a touch of an upward glide at the end—all while saying something close to "eeee-yaaaah-ee."

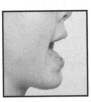

Open throat for a high nasal honk.

USES

Use this sound only when you desperately need attention, like when you are rooting for an underdog team, cheering on the floor of a political convention, signaling a waiter with attention deficit disorder, or want to be thrown out of class.

41

THE GOOSE HONK

Geese, who were once known for keeping to themselves, now seem to be the noisy tourists from the North, vacationing in parks, ponds, and public golf courses everywhere. Their now-familiar honks have transformed formerly pastoral fields into something akin to traffic jams in stadium parking lots. Their honks are distinct and spirited.

INSTRUCTIONS

1. Using the Basic Honk as a guide, begin in a strong falsetto voice (see the Falsetto, page 23) and then let it break suddenly into a low-voiced honk (see the Yodel, page 14). That will give you the familiar two-toned "haah-oonk" of the goose. Practice this.

Mouth and throat are opened wide.

2. Once you have this double-toned honk, try adding that peculiar, hollow resonance of a saxophone by raising your tongue slightly off the floor of your mouth. (See the Saxophone, page 122.)

Combine your Goose Honk with a Doppler change in pitch (see the Doppler Effect, page 135 and the Chicken Flutter, page 59) and you have a Canada goose flyby.

For the goose "phut-phut"—the sound that geese make as they graze the green grass of public parks— see the Splat, page 180. (The "phut-phut" is a nice, quiet bedtime effect for storybook geese in children's books.)

OCEAN LINER BLAST

T he Ocean Liner Blast is a rich, impressive (and realistic) sound that lends exotic mystery and intrigue to any get-together.

Blow through tight lips for a buzz and then add hum.

INSTRUCTIONS

1. Put your lips together fairly tightly in a very slight pucker.

2. Blow air through your lips to cause a slight vibration. Only the center of your lips (the portion where the upper and lower lips touch) should vibrate. Experiment with the tension of your lips and your blowing pressure.

3. Produce a low, resonant hum in your throat as you blow out air, to make your lips vibrate slightly. Try various pitches of humming to maximize the resonance of your lip buzz. (You're actually blending a deep vocal hum with a buzz of your lips, and the effect can be quite startling.)

USES

Your Ocean Liner Blast should sound exactly like the real thing. Use it to simulate cold, misty nights on the waterfront. If you let your hum fade away slowly, you will have the sound of a great luxury liner moored in the harbor distance. For a harbor medley, see the Seagull (page 82) and Whistling Wind (page 101). Or, listen to the CD to hear the Ocean Liner Blast introduce a sonic rendition of "Titanic: The Movie in 20 Seconds."

TUGBOAT BLAST

1 2 **3** 4

16

As they ply the waterways of our great harbors, tugboats signal to the world with their loud, comic blasts. Your Tugboat Blast can be a fine attention-getter—you can steal the show at parties or destroy the tedium of a dull sociology lecture.

Do not be discouraged if you can't make the tugboat sound immediately. It's not, by any means, an easy sound to master and will probably take several sessions. Be sure to listen to the CD.

INSTRUCTIONS

1. Poke out your lower lip and press it firmly over and against your tensed upper lip. The inside bottom of your lower lip should be held tightly against the outside edge of your upper lip. (If you glance in the mirror, and you look just a little like Sir Winston Churchill, you're on the right track.)

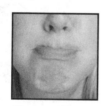

The lower lip protrudes over the upper lip, so its inside edge touches the tucked upper lip.

2. Blow air out so that the bottom lip vibrates in a kind of dirty "raspberry" sound (see page 171). You may find it helpful to concentrate the vibration slightly to one side of your mouth. Practice until you can produce an irritatingly constant buzzerlike sound. If it comes out a bit shaky at first, that's okay. Your hum, to come, will help stabilize and reinforce it.

3. Now add a strong, low hum registering at the same pitch of your lip buzz to create a loud, controlled blast. You may tense your lips and blow harder to increase the pitch of your buzz, or relax your lips a bit and reduce air pressure to lower the buzz.

Hum and blow out, vibrating your lower lip.

USES

After you are able to produce a strong blast, try challenging yourself to make the classic two-tone tugboat horn. To do it, produce a very high blast followed immediately by a very low blast. Cup your hands over your mouth to muffle the sound a bit.

The Tugboat Blast can be extremely useful in a "clear out, I'm coming through!" sort of way. It's also useful in situations involving the lifting and/or transport of heavy cargo (such as a friend's suitcase, a bag of fertilizer, or an over-sized toddler).

The combined hum and buzz necessary for the Tugboat Blast is a very versatile sound. You can adapt the basic hum and buzz so that it becomes: (1) a fire alarm, (2) a penalty buzzer, or (3) the signal for a game show strikeout on, say, *Family Feud*. It is also the basis for the Fuzz 'n' Funk Bass Guitar (see page 113).

CHAPTER 4

ANIMAL SOUNDS

Even if we didn't grow up against a bark-and-meow backdrop of pets, even if we don't live within earshot of a barnyard, we are all subjected to an array of animal sounds through Hollywood's vision of the world. What would Tarzan be without the chant of exotic birds, the howl of monkeys, and the roar of lions? What self-respecting movie about rural America could there be without crickets filling the evening air? And who could imagine a classic spring romance without birds twittering under soft dialogue?

Animal sounds set the stage. They create a mood. They surprise and entertain. They can give that dull office party, PTA meeting, airport waiting area, camp weenie roast, or classroom just the lift it needs. One well-timed fly impression can transform a tepid tea party into a tear-your-clothes-off toga bash.

THE PRINCIPLES OF ANIMAL SOUNDS

You can best approximate the vocal resonances of many different animals by producing sounds as you *inhale*—this is quite different from the normal speech produced when you *exhale*. Try speaking the first few letters of the alphabet in a normal voice. Then speak the first few letters, this time inhaling as you speak each one.

The inhaled voice sounds different from your normal voice and may be difficult to control at first. Practice saying short sentences in this "back talk," and then try singing high notes down to low notes. Production of these inhaled low notes is important for many of the animal sounds that follow.

THE STANISLAVSKY SCHOOL OF ANIMAL ACTING

The Stanislavsky method of animal acting holds that if you wish to sound like an animal, you must move like one and think like one. (Rumor has it that Stanislavsky himself enjoyed woodchuck imitations, on his haunches, in the privacy of his woodshed.)

For many, thinking like an animal is not difficult to do. Stand in front of a mirror. Imagine yourself as furry, hoofed, and horned. Now try to think like a cow about the pleasures of the pasture (meaning: *think grass*). You are big, slow, and not terribly bright. When you moo, *BE* the moo. All stupidity aside, such exercises will add depth and perspective to your animal.

When you make animal sounds, you have to totally commit. Lose your inhibitions. Mentally crawl inside the animal and use your entire body to act out the creature. When you do an elephant trumpet or dog bark, the difference between the reactions you elicit ("What a lame-o jerk . . ." and "Hey, cool . . .") is commitment.

FROM SQUEAKS TO ROARS . . .

Humans get pretty cocky as we sit atop the evolutionary heap with our sophisticated brain and voice mechanisms. Sure, plants are fairly quiet—the odd rustle here and there. But we often underestimate the subtlety, range, and flexibility of animal voices.

Take your basic chicken. Though not the Stephen Hawking of the animal kingdom, the chicken has a vocabulary of at least 28 different calls. The cheeping of hatching chicks, for instance, is used to communicate with others in the brood so that all the chicks emerge from their eggs at the same time. The rooster crows for his territory, while the mother hen clucks incessantly to keep her baby chicks together. There is a particular squawk to announce that an egg is laid and an excited cluck at feeding time. Almost all birds have equally complex (albeit more melodic) systems of vocal communication.

Most other animals, too, have evolved voices for communication. The Californian singing fish, for example, in a process similar to that of a croaking frog, uses a compartmentalized air bladder to produce a call underwater.

Many insects, and even fish, produce calls by rubbing parts of their bodies together in a process called *stridulation*. The very high-pitched, clicking sounds of grasshoppers and crickets can exceed man's range of hearing by almost five times.

Some animals, ranging from bats to porpoises, produce ultrasonic, high-frequency impulses in their throats or heads and then guide themselves by listening to the echoes of their own sounds. The animal world is noisy, indeed.

THE DOG BARK

Man's best friend? Well, not exactly. You may think of dogs simply as those furry little things that bark, lick your face, eat table scraps, and cost twenty bucks for the shots.

Well, that's all changed. Sometime during the yuppie years of the '80s, dogs (probably yuppie puppies) formed a union to upgrade their quality of life. The result is that highly bred designer dogs still bark and lick your face—at their convenience—but are now fed burger 'n' egg–flavored treats, cost hundreds of dollars, and roam safely behind invisible fences. These cagey canines have managed to market their big brown eyes very well.

You can go a long way with dog barks and whines. The sheer cuteness factor of imitation doggie barks is guaranteed to tug at the heart-strings of nearly everyone who hears them.

2. This time, do the same thing, but *inhale* as you say "err-ruff." Do you hear the difference? It sounds much more like the timbre of a dog. As you make the quick "err-ruff," your voice should rise very sharply in pitch. That's the Dog Bark.

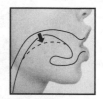

Tongue movement during "err-ruff."

INSTRUCTIONS

1. The Dog Bark is an animal sound that should be produced while inhaling. First, in a normal—but low—exhaled voice, make a long "rrrrr-ruff" sound. Bark with your exhaled rrrr-ruff's a few times. Err-ruff! Err-ruff! Err-ruff!

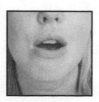

Inhale the bark through your slightly opened mouth.

3. Practice, keeping in mind how your favorite pooch greets you. To imitate large vicious dogs, lower the pitch of the "errr-ruff," pulling it farther down in your throat. For the yap-yap of those pesky smaller dogs (the ones with rhinestone collars and fur like feathers), raise the pitch of the bark and produce it high in your throat.

Surgeon General's Warning:

Bark at your own risk, and at small dogs only. Barking at Dobermans and pit bulls may cause unsightly puncture wounds.

USES

The Dog Bark has two basic uses. One is the create-havoc-in-the-classroom bark. A Dog Bark in any location where dogs are traditionally frowned upon is sure to divert attention away from the subject at hand—be it a pop quiz or a violin concert.

The second use of the bark is to torment unsuspecting dogs. With all the power that dogs wield in our homes, this seems to be poetic justice. As a little mutt is resting quietly, produce a quick bark. Nine times out of ten, the dog will immediately bounce to its feet and rush to the door or window. You have every right to feel smug.

The Stealth Bark

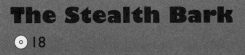

⊙ 18

An excellent technique, drawn from ventriloquism (see page 208), is to inhale the Dog Bark way back in your mouth, deeply into your throat, keeping your mouth just barely open. The sound becomes muffled and distant, and will totally confound the yappy schnauzer of the elderly lady riding in the elevator with you.

THE PUPPY WHINE

A s far as getting what you want is concerned, the Puppy Whine is the next best thing to begging on your knees. A much underused sound, the Puppy Whine is quite easy.

INSTRUCTIONS

1. Close your mouth and, in your finest and highest falsetto, make a short series of whining sounds. For each whine, start very high, and then let the whine slide down a few notes in pitch.

2. Widen your eyes and furrow your brow.

USES

The Puppy Whine is sure to melt the hardest of hearts—especially the female variety. Kids can whine for extra cookies from Mom. Secretaries can whine for higher raises, and dewy-eyed suitors can whine for more *amour* . . . or the remote control. Use along with pleading-dog eyebrows for added effect. Certainly the Whine is more elegant than pleading, and it gets you extra credit for originality.

Bayin' in the Distance
◉ 18

E ven if you've never lived in a bayou and let the dawgs out at night to hunt for raccoons, you can do a pretty good impression. Inhale the dog bark, pulling it way back into your mouth, making a nearly continuous series of "err-roh, er-roh" sounds in varying pitches. Done right, it'll get you a Moon Pie and Co'cola.

This sound of dogs baying in the distance can be used in combination with the French Horn (see page 119) for a hunting call, and horse gallops from the Triple Click (page 36) to create a Virginia Fox Hunt.

THE CAT MEOW

There are two kinds of people in the world: people who divide people into two kinds, and those who don't. And then, there are cat lovers; those people among us—and you know who you are—who project all manner of affection and personalities onto those temperamental throw pillows known as cats. Cat lovers cuddle, coddle, and cater to their cats, Little Friskying them to the point that they even leave cats their fortunes. But through it all, cats remain aloof, noncommittal, and arrogant, surfacing only occasionally from naps to acknowledge us with a soft "meow"—which in cat language translates as "drop dead."

That "meow" could more accurately be called "weow"—it's more precisely the sound that cats make. To capture the essence of cat, your "weows" must reflect a condescension, disinterest, and generally blasé attitude.

INSTRUCTIONS

The tongue is arched upward for added nasal tone.

1. With your highest falsetto, pronounce a soft, high-pitched "weow" that is very nasal. (If you hum a high note with your mouth closed, you will feel the sound high in your nasal passages. Use this nasal quality in your cat "weow.") The back of your tongue should be arched upward so that more sound is thrown into the nose.

2. Exaggerate and draw out the "weow" so that it's more like "we-owwww." (If you imagine that you are a bored teenager asking for money, you'll be close in attitude.)

USES

If you happen to be eloping by ladder, or simply need to gently wake a sleeping female, a soft cat "weow" makes a good signal. Cats do not wake males, especially snoring fathers. (The women tend to be the ones who rise and put the cat out.)

THE DONKEY BRAY

Donkeys catch a lot of flak, but their reputation for stubbornness is apparently well earned. You may not know this fact: In an average year, more people are killed from donkey-related deaths than from all the plane crashes in the world. That sobering fact must tell us something about air safety or donkey instability, but it's unclear what. In any case, it's an excellent party conversation starter or stopper, particularly if you finish it off with the following donkey impression.

INSTRUCTIONS

1. In a deep, gravelly voice, exhale a strong "aah-awww."

2. Then immediately on your inhale, say "eeeeh" in a high voice. (See the Inhaled Glottal Fry, page 27.) A few attempts will make you into a perfect jackass.

An alternate way of creating a donkey or mule sound—one learned from a professional mule handler—is to first whistle a loud taxi whistle (see the Fingerless Whistle, page 96), immediately followed by a strong exhaled "Ah-aaw." So your donkey call becomes a rhythmic "thweet-Ahaaw . . . thweet-Ahaaw . . . thweet-Ahaaw." ⦿ 20

USES

Kick off your next all-American political fundraiser with a Democratic Donkey Bray or a Republican Elephant Trumpet (page 72). It'll rattle the ice cubes and rock the vote.

THE COW MOO

Cows are not bright. For higher vertebrates, they are considered slow learners. This is the reason you never see trained circus cows on tricycles. No. Cows are milk machines, content to laze around in the sun and chew grass. Knowing this, your cow imitations should reflect this slow, accepting, bovine attitude.

Contrary to cherished myths, cows do not really "moo." They have no "m" sound. Cows really say "ooo," but kindergarten teachers and children's authors have plotted during the years to keep this from the public.

INSTRUCTIONS

1. Keep your mouth closed. Hum a moderately low, strong tone.
2. Keeping your mouth closed, think of a low "ooo" sound as you hum. Let the "ooo" rise and fall in pitch, and then trail off at the end like, "ooo-OOO-ooooo . . ."—just as a good Guernsey would.

USES

It is appropriate to moo politely before you down a glass of milk, or whenever you find yourself herded into a line such as at the theater, a concert, or the football season opener. Like our friend the cow, be sure to wear a vacuous smile and stare vacantly into space when you moo.

Very few males in our society, while driving past a roadside herd of grazing cows, can resist the mooing opportunity that it represents. Deep genetic urges take over—a kind of mammalian herding instinct. They will roll down the window, stick their lips to the wind, and "mmmoooooo" at the cows. It simply behooves them (or be-hoofs them, as the case may be) to do it. Although few cows find this at all amusing, mooing opportunities are difficult to resist.

THE PIG SQUEAL

Pigs are overweight because they eat constantly and are not under pressure to fit into swimsuits. They root and snort around in mud with other pigs, and they bask in the sun on off days. Not a bad life really, albeit cut short by the smokehouse.

But no pig with an ounce of porcine pride has ever uttered an "oink." Oink? An "oink" sounds more like the charming call of some long-legged bird than the snort of a 400-pound ham. No. Pigs grunt and squeal "ooo-wee."

INSTRUCTIONS

1. Produce the Inhaled Glottal Fry (see page 27).
2. As you make a deep and resonant inhaled fry, shape your mouth so that you pronounce a

Mouth shaped like "o" to add resonance.

slow "ooo-wee." Repeat over and over, shortening and quickening the pace of the "ooo-wees."
3. Once you are comfortable with the "ooo-wees," vary their loudness and pacing. Occasionally emphasize and hold the "wee" longer; at other times, emphasize the "ooo."
As you pronounce the "wee," let your Inhaled Glottal Fry rise in pitch for a more real-istic squeal. Work toward a series of sporadic and varying "ooo-wees."

USES

Pig snorts are always fine form just as you sit down at the table for dinner, and during the meal they lend an air of festive abandon.

If you really want to embrace your Pig Squeal, get down on all fours and lower your head to root around under sofa cushions or bedcovers.

All of us have, at one time or another, been chastised by our mothers or teachers for a room or desk that looks like a pigsty. Maybe now you have an appropriate response.

THE PIG SNORT

1 2 3 4

22

There are two particularly disgusting snorts you can use to spice up your pig impressions. Each uses your soft palate, the soft tissue in the back of the roof of your mouth that can close off the nasal passages from the throat. (See the Vocal Mechanism, page 2.)

INSTRUCTIONS

SNORT METHOD ONE ⊙22

Take a mouthful of air and close your mouth. Breathing independently through your nose, lips sealed, tense your cheeks to push the mouth air back and up into your nasal passages—the soft palate will make a disgusting fart-like sound inside your head. Yowzer. Now that's bacon.

A close-mouthed snort.

SNORT METHOD TWO ⊙22

Draw in air through your nose and make a loud snoring sound, as if you were your dad, Sunday afternoon, dozing on the sofa— one of those shake-the-window-pane snores. There's your Snort. Shorten it into a series of quick, disgusting wet snorts, and you've got it. Happy snortin'.

An open-mouthed snoring snort.

THE CHICKEN CLUCK

Chickens have blessed us with feathers for our pillows, eggs for our omelets, and drumsticks for Colonel Sanders. We have chicken jokes, chicken cartoons, chicken toys, and chicken tetrazzini.

And yet, in spite of their noble self-sacrifice, we find chickens funny. You want comedy? Throw a rubber chicken on stage.

The Chicken Cluck is the sound for attention-getting. It is as essential for party pranksters as rubber chocolates and whoopee cushions.

INSTRUCTIONS

1. With a nasal falsetto, make a "bok, bok, bok" sound. Keep your cheeks loose and, as you produce each "bok," allow your loose cheeks to fill with air and then collapse. The "boks" should have a sort of hollow, percussive sound.

2. After you master the "boks," add a "bok-ahhk" to the end. Let your voice soar up in pitch on the final "ak." Vary the pace of your "bok, boks" so that some are drawn out—way out—and others are clipped.

Allow cheeks to puff out loosely . . .

USES

The classic chicken impression is for anyone who attends raucous birthday bashes, Saturday-night fraternity parties, and out-of-control backyard barbecues. Bend your arms and insert your thumbs into your armpits. These are your chicken wings. Arch your back, throw out your chest, and turn your head from side to side in short jerky motions. Make your Chicken Cluck and scratch at the ground with your feet. *Bok-ahhk!* To become a rooster, pull a pair of red gym shorts over the top of your head.

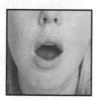

. . . and then collapse.

CHICKEN FLUTTERS

To add fright and flight to your chicken, you need to add fluttering to your clucks and "bok-ahhks." (Chicken Flutters are almost identical to the Helicopter whirs, page 144.)

INSTRUCTIONS

1. Tuck your lips inward so that they cover the upper and lower teeth. (You will look like a toothless Wal-Mart greeter.)

2. Close your mouth almost entirely, allowing a small opening between your tucked lips.

Lips tucked in over teeth.

3. Draw air in through the little opening, as you rapidly run the tip of your tongue up and down across the inward-protruding edges of your lips to produce the "flutter" of wings. If your sound is breathy and a trifle sloppy, so much the better, as chickens aren't exactly jet pilots. *Bok-ahhk!*

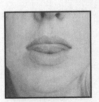

Tongue flutters up and down across inner lips.

THE PIGEON COO

Pigeons are technically called Rock Doves. They are native to gray rock cliffs in the mountains of eastern Europe—hence the mottled gray coloring and the penchant for tall, stone buildings in cities.

Stout birds, they stroll and peck in parks and other public places around the world. They hang out on rooftops and window ledges and congregate at the feet of old ladies. Among fowl, pigeons have become the urban welfare recipients. From their refined and respected cousins, the doves, pigeons inherited a lovely, sophisticated "coo." The Pigeon Coo has come to be one of the warmest and most congenial animal voices.

INSTRUCTIONS

1. Make a soft "ooo" sound in a breathy and moderately high falsetto. Repeat this "ooo" in rapid fashion.

2. To really sound pigeonlike, produce a tongue-flutter with the "ooo." The tongue-flutter is made the same way one rolls an "r" in Spanish—by placing the tongue on the roof of the mouth and blowing out air over the tongue so that it flutters. Practice this flutter.

Lips shaped for an "ooo" sound.

3. Combine the soft "ooo" and the tongue-flutter to make a muffled "cooo." The tongue-flutter can be continuous, but let the coos rise and fall in a series.

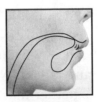

Tongue-flutter is added to the falsetto "ooo."

USES

If there was ever a sound of affection, this is it. You have no doubt seen birds "bill and coo." (Due to a pronounced lack of lips, birds "bill" instead of kiss.) As they bill, they coo showers of affection on each other.

You can do the same thing. Run your beak against the neck of an acquaintance and "coo" softly—guaranteed either to start or stop a friendship very quickly.

BIRD TWEETS, ETC.

Birds offer up their little voices all around us. They whistle, chatter, squawk, and talk with magical ease. Whether marking territory or calling out for a date, they are all part of a great conversation.

Most animals just give you a dirty look if you imitate them, but not birds. They will respond, rewarding you instantly with chirpy dialogue—the ultimate compliment for a sound maker. (The trick is figuring out what you just said to the bird.)

INSTRUCTIONS

1. For little bird tweets, use the Invisible Whistle (see page 92). Because you produce this whistle *inside* your mouth, your lips are free to articulate the whistle into little tweets and chirping sounds.
2. As you whistle, move your lips slightly as if you are saying "bree, bree, bree," and you will hear little birds. (This is the sound of circling cartoon birds after Elmer Fudd gets slammed over the head with a mallet.)

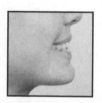

Lips pulled back to say "bree."

BIRD CHIRPS ⊙25

This is a simple one that really sounds like the chirps of little hopping house wrens, but it will take a day or so to build up the muscles to do it.
1. Listen to the CD. These chirps are created by forming a bubble of air between the top of your flattened tongue and the front roof of your mouth.

2. Keep your mouth almost closed. Press your tongue against the roof of your mouth, forcing the air to squeak out the front of your mouth. It will sound like air seepage at first, but after a little trial and error you can learn to channel the air tightly into a distinct chirp. With this chirp perfected, you can attract birds in parks and chat with parakeets.

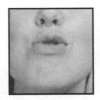

Sides of tongue sealed against roof of mouth.

BIRD SQUAWKS ⊙ 25

Squawks are very expressive and flamboyant bird-speak, usually uttered by larger birds . . . or little birds with bad 'tude. Here's how you create them:

1. Inhale and say the word "err-rah" in a high, nasal voice. (For help with inhaled talk, see the Inhaled Glottal Fry, page 26, and Back Talk, page 203.)

2. Practice this until it sounds very nasal, and you can elongate the "err-raaaaah."

3. Vary the length of your squawk and change the pitch up and down to sound like different birds.

For the Birds: The Universal Bird Call

This works well among avid birders, at a backyard barbeque, or an office outing, or on a school field trip. Announce that you have just learned a universal bird call that communicates with any species of bird. You will attempt to do this call, but you must have silence. You flex and limber up your fingers, loosen your jaw and head, maybe even jump up and down to warm up and get ready. Make a brief show of your preparation. Bringing your cupped fingers to your mouth slowly, announce: "Ladies and gentlemen, the universal bird call!" Pause . . . clear your throat . . . vamp a bit . . . then . . . take in a huge breath of air and yell . . . "Hey, you—with the feathers. Yeah, you. Get over here!" Works every time. Although birds remain oblivious, your audience will, in fact, think your call is clearly "for the birds."

GENERIC JUNGLE BIRD 1 2 **3** 4 ⊙

A variation on the Peacock Wail—one that, by the way, sounds fabulous echoing down a school or office hallway—is the Generic Jungle Bird. This is a kind of loud kookaburra call that you hear in nearly every Hollywood jungle/adventure movie ever made. And it's not a jungle bird at all—it's some guy with cupped hands crouching in the bushes.

INSTRUCTIONS

1. To do this, first you have to do a machine gun rat-a-tat. Imagine an eight-year-old doing the "eh-eh-eh-eh-eh" of a machine gun—it's actually a series of glottal stops, staccato and rapid. (It has the same feeling as the "ha-ha-ha-ha-ha" of laughter.) Do this a few times.

2. Now, here's the trick: Shape your mouth like an O and use a nasal, falsetto voice to do the same "machine-gun-glottal stop." Practice a bit to refine it, and call out an open-throated "oooo-Waaaaa-oooo." It's a passable Generic Jungle Bird.

3. But if you really want your call to soar to the ceiling, do the following: *Inhale* and do the same thing. Yes, you can do it. It will feel really strange at first—but, hey, YOU are strange, or you wouldn't be reading this. Work on it. The quality becomes totally birdlike (see the Inhaled Glottal Fry, page 27) and will blow people away. . . . oooo-Waaaaa-oooo!

THE PEACOCK WAIL

Peacock wails are an excellent jungle effect. When you hear just this sound, you think, my, that's a bird of a different color. You think Tarzan, you think *exotique*, you think Travel Channel.

INSTRUCTIONS

1. To create your own peacock mating calls, call—in a high, open-mouthed, nasal, sirenlike voice—the sounds "aaah-AAA-aaaah, aaah-AAA-aaaah, aaah-AAA-aaaah," in rhythmic swells.

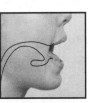

Tongue arched, mouth open wide.

2. Cup your hands over your mouth like a megaphone. It not only gives the call interesting timbre, but makes you stand out in line at Starbucks.

USES

Proud as a peacock—now you have a sonic blast of a wail to match the strut. So spread your feathers, and give a wave and a wail at that attractive bird across the bar. Though this technique won't guarantee you a date, it will undeniably get you attention.

THE CRICKET CHIRP

Crickets form Mother Nature's little glee club. Their evening sing-alongs fill the air with chirping music that has soothed more people to sleep than Brahms's lullaby. The sound of crickets has come to be the epitome of a peaceful, country night, and is a becoming ambience for a story.

INSTRUCTIONS

1. Form your mouth as in the Pucker Whistle (see Whistles, page 89). Practice until you can *inhale* through the pucker to make a clear whistle.

2. Work up a fair amount of saliva in your mouth. Tilt your head forward so that the pucker points downward.

3. As you inhale a clear whistle, adjust your tongue so that the air coming into your mouth (through the small opening of your pucker) bubbles through the saliva on your tongue. The bubbling of your inhaled whistle produces the rapid chirps of a cricket.

Inhaled air over saliva breaks a whistle into chirps.

Nature Knowledge #73:

At your next backyard barbecue, lob this into the conversational mix: Mention that by counting the number of chirps a cricket makes in 15 seconds and adding 40 to your total, you can come within a degree or so of determining the outside temperature in degrees Fahrenheit. (For Celsius, count the number of chirps in 8 seconds and add 5.) Yes, you can explain, cricket metabolism and consequent chirp rate varies proportionately with the temperature.

4. Practice. Stop for a while, and come back to it again until you get it. The saliva should be kept between the middle of your tongue and the roof of your mouth. The air bubbling through it should keep it from moving too far toward the front of the mouth. Some people use the same bubbling technique, but whistle normally (exhaling), and tilt the head upward to bubble the tongue saliva. Either way, produce the cricket chirps in gentle waves of sound by whistling in rhythmical swells.

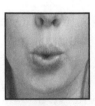

Puckered lips produce inhaled whistle.

USES

If you ever need to set the mood of the great outdoors for a story or play, try the Cricket Chirp. It's also a fine effect in response to some bone-headed idea at a meeting—a lone Cricket Chirp is a comic placeholder for silence and lack of enthusiasm. "Are you with me, folks?!" (beat) Your response: Lone cricket chirp. The sound can be so realistic that you can actually convince your teacher that the little creatures are loose in algebra class.

Of course, the natural time for cricket chirps is at night. Cut off the lights, sit in a warm tub, and create your own pond. Get that special someone to produce the Frog Croak (see page 74) and you can have your own romantic, secluded lagoon.

Insect "Loud Mouths"

Insects are able to produce a dazzling range of sounds, from the quiet whine of mosquitoes to the chattering buzz of grasshoppers. But the supreme vocalist of the insect world is the cicada, or seventeen-year locust. The male cicada sings in a loud, shrill buzz, produced by rapid contractions of a powerful muscle that causes a hard plate to vibrate. The resultant "sexual buzz" is used to attract female cicadas from miles around, transforming the local park into a huge insect singles bar.

THE FLY BUZZ

Buzzes are irritating. Alarm clocks buzz. Electric razors buzz. Dentists' drills buzz. There are buzzers to alert you, warn you, and pester you. There are penalty buzzers to tell you when you're wrong. There is something menacing in that jagged little metallic hum that penetrates deeply and provokes those who hear it.

But of all the disquieting buzzes around us, the most irritating is the buzz of the common housefly. Ounce for ounce, the housefly has a greater ability to ruffle our composure than any other speck of matter in the universe. That is exactly why the Fly Buzz is so much fun—you can bug the heck out of folks with it. The Fly Buzz strikes a primal nerve in almost everyone.

INSTRUCTIONS

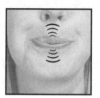

Taut lips vibrate with high buzz.

1. Press your lips together tightly.
2. Blow air out through your lips so that the center of your lips vibrates with a high buzz. This requires some experimentation. (Try tightening your lips in such a way that only the inner edges of the upper and lower lips vibrate—not the whole lips.)
3. Once you get a consistent humming buzz, note that if you tighten your lips, the vibration rises in pitch; if you allow your lips to relax more, the pitch drops. For the Fly Buzz, you need a very high, thin buzz. (The humming buzz of bees, locusts, and electric shavers is somewhat lower.) Practice until you develop a clear, controlled buzz.

THE FLY IMPRESSION ⊙28

Flies have never figured out window glass. We all know that tormenting, persistent "fizz" they make as they struggle endlessly to fly through it. You can make that sound by producing your high buzz and then moving your lower jaw slightly but rapidly, up and down. This changes the tension of your lips so that the buzz is broken into the scuffing sound of fly-against-glass.

Now, for the fly takeoff, bend your elbows and, palms down, raise your hands up to the level of your shoulders. Rapidly flap these little hand-wings as you buzz. Doing your Fly Buzz, flit about the room, using short, quick steps.

This is the basic fly. Continue to flit, tilting and veering until you come to open wall space.

When it is time to land, face the wall and buzz your way right into it. Just as you hit, raise your right arm and leg slightly to one side and flatten against the wall. (You will be balancing against the wall on one foot.) This gives the impression that you are adhering to the wall with your little suction feet. Stay motionless, for a long, uncomfortable moment, and then, while still flat, nervously clean your face with your hands, just as a housefly might.

As you can imagine, this impression goes over well at senior proms, office parties, stately art openings, and even in elevators. With the Fly Buzz alone, it is possible to irritate up to forty people at one time.

But be careful. Someone might follow your act with their impression of a gigantic fly swatter.

THE LION GROWL

Lions are the superstars of the animal kingdom. With their impressive, punked-out
hairdos, they have starred in innumer-
able B-grade movies, television series, and PBS
documentaries. Although they tend to shy away
from comedy roles, their heavy, dramatic parts
have earned them star status. Your Lion Growl
should always reflect this tradition of prideful
showmanship.

INSTRUCTIONS

1. Make the Inhaled Glottal Fry (see page 27).
Open your throat wide to make the deepest and
most resonant sound you can. Shape your mouth
to make an "rrr" sound as you inhale, raising the
back of the tongue upward to constrict the upper
throat a bit. This will pull the "rrr" sound back
farther in the upper throat.

2. Shift from this inhale "rrr" to
an inhaled "o" sound. You will
have to drop the floor of your
mouth and open your throat
wider. To develop a roar, start
with the growl on a higher note.
As you move from an "rrr" to an
"o" sound, let your growl slide to
lower notes.

*Arched tongue
moving
downward
during growl.*

USES

Lion Growls can be combined with Elephant
Trumpets (page 72), Bird Squawks (page
63), and Monkey Chatter (page 71) for
your own portable jungle scenes.
　Because your lion roars and growls are
made far back in your mouth and throat, they
will have a slightly distant sound to them; try
using them during a telephone call. Roar, scream,
and then hang up. Wait for the return call.

MONKEYS AND SUCH

Monkeys, chimpanzees, apes, and baboons are our second cousins. And we treat them like second cousins— we can't keep their names straight. In truth, they are wildly different animals with wildly different voices, which means, in a vocal sense, that you can do just about any voice and it will sound right.

INSTRUCTIONS

1. Pucker your lips and make the sound of a big, cartoon kiss. Practice this sound until you get a loud squeal.

Slightly puckered lips with air pulled in and out.

2. Breathing through your nose, push your tongue forward and backward, pushing air in and out of your puckered lips. Vary the sound by loosening your lips. It will begin to sound like a clamoring troop of monkeys— or office workers on coffee break.

For more variations, inhale and exhale similar squeals made on fleshy body parts, such as the back of a hand. Careful trying this on others. Such monkeying around can attract lawsuits. . . .

THE CHIMP ⦿ 30

For an excited chimp, pooch out your lips in an O shape, and exhale and inhale the sound "ooo" at varying speeds, in lower and higher voices.

Inhale and exhale excited chimp "oooh."

Crouch beside, say, your mother, poke through her hair, pick off a bug, make some chimp "ooo's," and then mime eating the bug, and you'll be asked to leave the table. Family preening is, however, a bonding moment.

ELEPHANT TRUMPET

1 2 **3** 4

31

This pachydermal pucker is a surefire hit at chic get-togethers, office parties, and Republican conventions. A quick series of elephant trumpets is guaranteed to stop conversation dead as the room braces itself for something else to happen—either an elephant charge . . . or your boss firing your butt.

INSTRUCTIONS

1. Your lips should be dry and free of all lipstick, suntan lotion, and motor oil. Tuck your lips in, with the upper lip slightly over the lower lip. Keep lips very taut.

2. Fill your cheeks with air so that they, and the areas above and below your lips, billow out. (The corners of your mouth should be held in tightly, as if you're trying to create dimples.)

3. Allow your upper lip to billow out slightly more than your lower lip. Forcefully blow out air so that the lips vibrate, making a squealing sound. Continue to try variations, working to produce a full-sounding trumpet that rises and falls in pitch—exactly like an elephant cry.

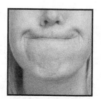

Taut lips held in tightly.

Allow areas above and below lips to billow.

72

4. The sound alone is not enough, however. You must add realistic trunk action. With your arm extended, place the inside of your elbow next to the side of your face. As you sound the elephant call, raise and lower your head and arm, in the manner of a rogue bull elephant.

It's unclear exactly what you are signaling in elephant-ese—this has not been field-tested—but probably something like, "Hey, big girl, what's your sign? . . ."

The Four-Eared Elephant

Recent research has discovered that an elephant's trumpet generates two sounds: the familiar call we hear through the air, and a second, ultra-low–frequency infrasound that travels through the ground as a seismic wave. Other elephants hear the sound waves, from distances up to 20 miles, with their—wait for it—feet, particularly their toenails. This helps them communicate movements over great distances with their own and other herds. As we know, elephants have big ears, but not so much as hearing aids but more as radiators for cooling themselves down.

USES

You can add dimension to your elephant calls by grunting a Tarzanlike "Ungowa, Nimba" (ün gòw´a nǐmba) before each trumpet. And herds of elephants become a reality with five or more elephant callers. Imagine the fun of trampling your friend's living room in a frenzied stampede.

73

THE FROG CROAK

1 2 3 4

32

The frog is undoubtedly the most lovable amphibian. But frogs suffer from bad press. Okay, sure, they're cold and clammy, but they're not slimy, and it's not their fault they've been used to chase countless schoolgirls. And frogs don't give you warts—they have clearer skin than high-school sophomores.

In reality, frogs, along with toads, do a lot more than croak—they have some of the most sonically rich animal calls in nature, with many accents and dialects. Many of the sounds we hear in the evening that we assume are coming from birds or insects are actually emanating from frogs and toads of all sizes. In amphibian language, they are actually at a huge singles party, yelling "Date me! Date me!"

Frogs and toads have an amazing range of territorial and mating calls: the chirps of tiny "peepers" in early spring; the rusty-hinged groans of pickerel frogs in early summer; to the long, high trills of the American toad in mid-summer; to late summer's thunderous bull frog "Giga-Rumps." Different types of frogs and toads are triggered to begin calling at different temperatures, so they don't all call at once and drown one another out.

The frog croak here is a sort of cartoon version of several frog and toad sounds.

INSTRUCTIONS

1. Shape your mouth as if you were going to sing the very lowest "o" sound that you can. Your throat should be very open and your lips in an O shape.

Throat opened and mouth shaped like an O to add resonance.

2. Exhale a low "o" sound, then inhale the same low "o" sound to produce a very hollow, resonant, but almost crackly sound. Practice this deep, guttural inhaled croak.

3. As you inhale the low tone, keep your throat very open and articulate a "rah" with your mouth. Draw the "rah" out longer to sound more like a frog, and, as you draw out the inhaled "raaaah," let the pitch of your croak glide upward just slightly. Try stringing several of these "wahs" together without stopping the croaking tone.

With some practice you should sound more and more like a frog. Once you have mastered the basic croak, you can do several frog variations. To make the classic "ribit" sound, produce your inhaled croaking sound and just inhale the word "ribit." Then try other frog favorites, such as "breep" and "nee-deep."

USES

The Frog Croak should be used with some discretion, for it can easily be mistaken for an attack of gas. Try hunkering down into a crouch on all fours. Croak, and then lap your tongue out quickly a few times. You might try a Fly Buzz (see page 68) while tracking the fly with your frog eyes; then suddenly let your tongue snap out for a quick catch, eat, and swallow.

Party Game: Animal Charades

A fine party icebreaker for young and old is the game Animal Charades. Cover animal crackers with aluminum foil. Each guest selects one from a bowl, unwraps it privately, and then acts out the animal he's chosen. When the others, working individually or in teams, guess the animal, the performer gets to eat the animal cracker. It's a great game for adults to play with kids, because kids, nearly always, have the edge.

THE DUCK QUACK

Everyone needs a quack in her repertoire, if only to sing "Old McDonald Had a Farm." (The use of past tense in the song has always been troubling. Was the farm repossessed by the bank? It gives one pause . . . but I digress.) Here's how to make a wise quack that will turn a duck's head.

INSTRUCTIONS

1. Close your mouth, with your upper and lower teeth nearly together.

2. Place your tongue flat in your mouth, firmly against the back of your teeth and slightly between your upper and lowers, especially toward the back of your mouth.

3. Now push air out the back sides of your mouth, over or under your tongue. You should hear a rubbery, quacking sound. There's your quacker.

4. You need a lot of pressure to make a good, crisp quack. First push air from your lungs and force it to the back of your mouth, above the back of your tongue. Now, by pushing your throat and back of your tongue sharply upward against the roof of your mouth, squeeze this air out the sides of your mouth. Experiment. You will begin to feel it. QUACK. (You will find that once you get the hang, you can quack and still breathe normally through your nose.)

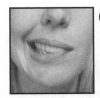

Push air out back and side of mouth.

Keep your cheeks loose. With your cheek muscles, and your cupped hands, you can affect everything from a near-perfect duck call to a silly cartoon quack. Try saying something like "bu-eee, bu-ee, bu-ee" out the side of your mouth as you quack. Quack on.

USES

For a little challenge, try an effect called "Double Duck Danube." ⊙34 You can do an awesome rendition of Strauss's "Blue Danube" waltz by creating *two* duck quacks at one time—an impressive feat, by any standard. Once you have accomplished the Duck Quack on one side of you mouth, try it on the other. Having done that, now do a quack, simultaneously, on both sides of your mouth. You're off.

Try the "Blue Danube" or any slow, languid song, doing a duck on one side of your mouth, answering with the other side, and then doing both. You can even do harmony. Push the envelope. Try Jimi Hendrix's "Purple Haze."

The sound of Double Ducks is incredibly irritating to others but wonderfully fulfilling.

THE TURKEY GAA-LAA

The turkey has been a prominent symbol in the United States since the first Thanksgiving. It represents the noblest of American traditions—hard work and eating 'til it hurts. Ben Franklin even lobbied for it to become the national bird.

More recently, however, the turkey has come to be associated with anything that false starts, misfires, runs over budget, or otherwise "fowls" up. All the more reason to use the Turkey Gaa-laa these days!

INSTRUCTIONS

1. Say "gaa-laa, gaa-laa" in a nasal falsetto. This is your fundamental turkey sound.
2. Place the index finger and thumb of one hand gently on either side of your larynx (Adam's apple) about midway up your neck.

Massage the Adam's apple rapidly.

3. As you say "gaa-laa," rapidly (but gently) vibrate the larynx with an up-and-down motion of the hand. This will give a quick vibrato effect. Practice repeating "gaa-laa, gaa-laa-aaaaa" in quick succession. Let your voice trail off at the end, but continue your manual vibrato until the "gaa-laa" has completely stopped.

For an improved effect, try flopping your tongue rapidly between your lips to add tremolo.

USES

The "gaa-laa, gaa-laa" sound is probably the most effective and least subtle way to call someone a turkey. You can use the rallying cry to single out nerds, wimps, weenies, klutzes, creeps, and bozos whose actions qualify them for Turkeydom.

THE LOON

Loons are magnificent sound creatures. Their echoing calls vary from warbling laughter to plaintive, heart-touching wails. Out of the many calls they perform, here are two:

INSTRUCTIONS

THE WAIL

1. The Loon Wail is done exactly like the Seagull (see page 82), only long and as sad-sounding as possible. It is simply one long yodel of a cry.

THE WARBLE

Young sopranos can often do a perfect laughing loon warble—"ha-ha-ha-Ha-HA-Ha-ha"—but few of us are young sopranos. You can come close by using the Fingerless Whistle (see page 96).
1. As you do the Fingerless Whistle, place your index finger just below your bottom lip.

2. Jiggle your finger against your chin so that your whistle is warbled into the familiar "ha-ha-ha-Ha-HA-Ha-ha!" (Basically, you'll be doing the Spinning Tires, described on page 136, without the humming.)

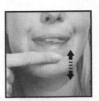

Add finger jiggle on chin to Fingerless Whistle.

THE DOLPHIN

Dolphins are perhaps the most beloved of all sea creatures. They are mammals, of course, and may well be smarter than humans—given that they live at the beach, and don't wear toupees, loud pants, or white shoes. They communicate in complex sounds and you can create some of them.

INSTRUCTIONS

CLICKS #1   ⊙37

Dolphins echolocate underwater for food and for protection against predators, and at marine parks for the enjoyment of overweight tourists. Now you can, too.

1. Flatten your tongue a bit, just letting it poke slightly through your teeth. (Your teeth should be resting lightly on the sides of your tongue.) Let the back of your tongue rest loosely against the back, left or right, inner cheek of your mouth.

Clicks produced, inhaled, between back of tongue and cheek.

2. Now, draw in air, around the front of the tongue on that side of your mouth, causing the tongue in the rear to vibrate against the cheek in a series of clicks.

3. Practice until you get controlled clicks. You are now echolocating.

CLICKS #2   ⊙37

Another method for making dolphin clicks is by inhaling clicks, much like you might do to create the sound of frog croaks (see the Inhaled Glottal Fry, page 26), except that as you inhale the croaks, keep your voice as high as possible, shaping the mouth and throat as if making "eee" and "aaah" sounds.

SQUEAKS AND CALLS   ⊙37

Dolphins do not naturally make those rubbery, buzzing, and squeaking sounds you hear in marine parks and movies. They are taught by humans to make them because we think it's cute. Dolphins have lungs like we do, but they breathe through an airhole in the top rear of their head. (Imagine humans smoking cigars through the tops of their heads.) Though they produce the sounds by squeezing the muscular flap of their airhole, they are taught to open their mouth—so we can imagine them "speaking" as we do.

INSTRUCTIONS

1. The very best dolphin squeaks are created by using the Vent Voice (see page 208) to add a munchkin quality to the sound. But a simple high falsetto (see Falsetto, page 23) will do.

Inhale with mouth, varying "eee" and "aaah."

2. Say something like "eeee-aaaah," slowly and repeatedly in a high voice or Vent Voice.

3. As you say the "eeee-aaaah," massage your Adam's apple up and down rapidly to get the quavering, dolphin sound.

Massage Adam's apple to add quaver.

USES

This is not a sound you'll find a lot of uses for except perhaps at fish restaurants, aquariums, and pool parties. Certainly, you can feel confident that, should you run into a dolphin, you could strike up a reasonable conversation.

THE SEAGULL

Cocktail party factoid: The Latin name of the black-headed seagull is *Larus ridibundus ridibundus*. Drop that into the conversational mix before your seagull impression, and folks may think you're not as stupid as you look.

INSTRUCTIONS

1. For a fine seagull, you need to do the Fingerless Taxi Whistle (see page 97).

2. Now close your fingers and thumb of one hand, as if you are grasping an imaginary pipe about the size of a toilet-paper tube. The circle made by your thumb and pointing finger is facing you.

3. Do the Fingerless Whistle into this rolled cup of your hand. Overblow your whistle a bit and you will hear a little yodel. There's your seagull. (The resonance of your hand causes the whistle to break.) Work at it, and it will become quite realistic. The rhythm should be something like "Daa-deeeee, dee-dee-dee-dee-dee" and trailing off.

USES

You can combine the Seagull with the Tugboat Blast and rising and falling whooshes of wind for an impressive harbor medley. ⊙27

THE FISH

Anyone can do a fine carp impression if they really put their mind to it. Here's your chance to show the world what you're made of.

INSTRUCTIONS

1. First, look in a mirror. Notice your eyes are a little bulgy? Maybe you should get your thyroid checked.

2. Begin and end your fish with the Aquarium Effect (see page 156). Stick out your jaw and pooch out your bottom lip. Open and close it slowly and rhythmically.

3. Place the palms of your hands on each side of your face (like a *Home Alone*

scream). From the front, pinky edge of your hand, open and close your hands like gill flaps, synchronizing the movement with that of your mouth. You're a fish.

USES

Turn that party into a great goldfish bowl. Demonstrate the Fish, and get everyone to do it with you . . . Wait. Don't stop reading yet. . . . Each person flaps his gills, opening and closing his mouth, and swims slowly, directly toward the face of another fish. Just as the faces almost touch, suddenly each fish veers away, and swims on toward another fish face. It is guaranteed to mix and moisten a party.

CHAPTER 5

WHISTLES

Whistles are the shrill signals of the world. They warn. They mark. They urge and entertain. The toy train whistles its way around the crouching six-year-old. The teakettle beckons us to the kitchen. Street-corner toughs two-finger whistle their approval of the passerby.

Whistles indicate authority. With a single whistle, factory workers mop their brow as clanking machinery is silenced. White-gloved policemen tame traffic with a frantic semaphore of waves and whistles. Lifeguards and pot-bellied gym teachers twirl their little silver symbols of power at the end of shoelace lanyards.

With a whistle, we summon the dog from our neighbor's flower bed. We whistle absentmindedly to kill time. We whistle while we work—the sonic signature of janitors and repairmen.

We whistle up our sagging courage, and whistle to ignore. By clasping our hands behind us, rocking on our heels and whistling, we feign innocence. Like no other single sound, the whistle graces us with its versatility.

WHISTLING WIZARDRY

Many of us consider whistling a musical novelty, best reserved for the privacy of basement, attic, and backyard. From time to time, we are all subjected to the overly cheerful public whistler who performs gratis in checkout lines, crowded buses, and bank lobbies. We hear the occasional whistler—the guy from the local tire dealership—in amateur talent nights. Whistling performances are viewed ascance mostly as talent misdirected or gone astray.

But over the years, the art of whistling has surfaced occasionally to bask briefly in the rays of the public limelight. In the early 1900s, vaudeville had its share of novelty whistlers. The great Al Jolson was a whistler of some renown.

In the 1930s a serious whistler, Fred Lowery, blew onto the scene. Practicing whistling for four or more hours a day, Lowery developed unheard-of muscular control and a musicianship uncommon to whistling. He teamed up with the orchestra of Horace Heidt in 1938 for a soulful rendition of "Indian Love Call" that sold well over a million records. Lowery went on to record works ranging from "Listen to the Mockingbird" to selections from Bach and Stravinsky.

In Walt Disney's 1938 classic film *Snow White and the Seven Dwarfs*, seven little men in drooping hats endeared themselves to the American public with their tight whistling harmonies. The song "Whistle While You Work" rocketed into the hit parade.

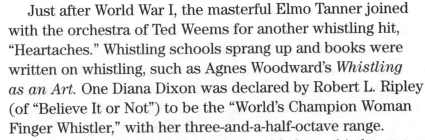

Just after World War I, the masterful Elmo Tanner joined with the orchestra of Ted Weems for another whistling hit, "Heartaches." Whistling schools sprang up and books were written on whistling, such as Agnes Woodward's *Whistling as an Art*. One Diana Dixon was declared by Robert L. Ripley (of "Believe It or Not") to be the "World's Champion Woman Finger Whistler," with her three-and-a-half-octave range.

Julie Andrews made her bid for world-class whistler status with her 1955 Broadway debut in the opening of *The Boy Friend*. In 1957, "The Colonel Bogey March" from the motion picture *The Bridge over the River Kwai* had more Americans whistling than any other song in history.

About this same time, the bittersweet theme from the television show *Lassie* introduced millions of misty-eyed viewers to the weekly adventures of a boy and his collie with an IQ of 140. Television gave us the homespun theme of *The Andy Griffith Show*, during which the folksy Griffith and his every-son, Opie, skip stones across a pond. About this same time, the genius of Toots Thielemans pulled whistling into the idiom of jazz, with his classic jazz guitar and whistle-piece "Bluesette."

Of course, whistling has had its novelty luminaries. Horatio Q. Birdbath whistled and made all manner of noises for Spike Jones's antic orchestrations of sound and music during a span of some twenty years. Simon Argevitch, a carnival and talk-show veteran, managed to eke out a whistle with nine cigars, five spoons, and six drinking straws in his mouth.

There are many serious whistlers, too. Among the best known is probably Roger Whitaker. The international baritone singer talked and occasionally whistled his way through a range of standards—folk and popular songs in the 1960s.

The International Whistlers Convention has been held annually since 1973 during the third or fourth week of April in Louisburg, North Carolina. Whistling enthusiasts from all over the world converge for world-class competition in several

different whistling categories, contributing to a mass, rubbery-lipped celebration of the noble folk art of whistling.

Whistling will wax and wane in popularity. It is an art form that bubbles up naturally in many forms in every culture. It may suddenly surface in the form of an elegant movie theme, a rap or rock diversion, or a folk-song revival. But there is no doubt: Those penetrating, piping, and mysteriously compelling tones of the whistle will always be with us.

THE WHISTLE PRINCIPLE: HOW WHISTLES WORK

The whistle has a characteristic rounded, clean tone that is marked by purity and simplicity. And yet the aerodynamics of whistle production are some of the most subtle and complex of any sound. Only recently have physicists begun to unravel its mysteries.

Almost every sound around us is created by the transfer of vibrations from some rapidly moving object to surrounding air molecules. In the case of the voice, our vocal folds vibrate, rhythmically compressing the air around them. The resulting vibrations travel in the air to the ears of others. In whistles, however, no physical object vibrates—the air molecules themselves vibrate directly.

All whistles, from puckers to piccolos, operate on the scientific principle that when a steady stream of air is disturbed in a particular manner, the turbulence produces a series of regularly spaced, swirling vortices of air. These spirals of air act as vibrating devices that produce the sharp whistle tone.

The pure whistle of a flute, for instance, is attributed to the fact that it is only the air particles themselves (and not reeds or strings) that vibrate to produce the remarkably ethereal, "airy" tone.

LEARNING WHISTLES

Whistles are the most difficult and evasive mouth sounds to learn—and they're maybe even more difficult to teach. Perhaps more than any other sound, mouth whistles require delicate manipulation of the tongue, teeth, lips, and sometimes fingers. For this reason, perfecting whistles requires more than the usual patience and practice to adapt the general rules to the peculiar structure of your own mouth.

Experimentation is necessary in developing your whistles. Adjust the lips. Try different air pressures. Move the tongue slightly. And always listen for hints of that elusive whistling sound. Don't get frustrated. It's a process. Take a break, and try again later.

Once you begin to hear a faint whistle, you are close to home. It will then be a matter of fine tuning.

Pucker Up

The Pucker Whistle is produced by a principle known as the "whole tone effect," the same principle by which teakettles whistle.

The whistle is generated when a flow of air rushes against a small hole. Spirals of air form around the outer edges of the hole, setting up rapid disturbances in the air flow. These minute eddies of air create sound vibrations as the air is forced through the opening, and a whistle tone is produced.

The loudness of the Pucker Whistle is determined by the speed of the airflow. Blowing harder makes a louder whistle.

The pitch (or how high or low the note is) is determined by the size of your mouth. Drawing the tongue back and lowering the floor of the mouth enlarges the mouth cavity and lowers the tone. Pushing the tongue forward and raising the floor of the mouth, on the other hand, shrinks the resonating mouth cavity and raises the pitch.

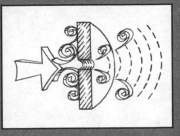

THE PUCKER

The Pucker Whistle is the most universal and useful member of the whistle family. Throughout history, everyone from barons to buffoons has used it to signal, summon, and give vent to melody. As a ritual of childhood, most of us spent hours hyperventilating to perfect his or her own elusive musical pucker.

INSTRUCTIONS

The Pucker Whistle comes quite naturally to some people but can be difficult for others. There are three basic variables involved: the tongue, the pucker, and the blowing of air.

1. Relax your tongue on the floor of your mouth, setting the front edge of it against the back of your bottom teeth.

2. Pucker your lips slightly. Do not exaggerate the pucker. All you really need to do is form a small round opening in the center, between the lips.

Pucker lips, being sure the hole between the lips is round.

3. Blow, gently—as if you were romantically blowing out a lighted match in front of your lips. Blowing hard only distorts the whistle.

If you have trouble producing a whistle, look in a mirror as you try. Open and close the small hole between your lips ever so slightly. Make it as round as possible. (Be sure your tongue is out of the way of the center hole.) Try tensing your lips into a more "pointed" pucker and vary your lip tension.

To lower the pitch, draw your tongue back slightly from the edge of your bottom teeth as you lower the floor of your mouth. To raise the pitch, keep the front of your tongue against the bottom teeth and arch the back and midportions of the tongue upward, pushing the tongue farther forward in your mouth. (It helps to imagine that you have water in your mouth. Raise and lower pitch by pushing the water out or holding more water.)

Try a musical scale and simple melodies, such as "Oh! Susannah" and "On Top of Old Smokey" before you go on to anything more complicated. Whistling is perfect for old standards and classical numbers but somehow lacks the "umph" necessary for rap, grunge, or heavy metal. (For sound effects using your Pucker Whistle, see the Hum and Whistle Multipurpose Space Effect, page 149.)

VIBRATO   ⊙ 38

In whistling, the difference between rank amateur and seasoned professional is all a matter of vibrato, that subtle wavering of a note that gives it fluidity—and schmaltz.

For Vibrato, allow the mid-part of your tongue to waver up and down.

To add vibrato to your whistle, keep your tongue against your bottom teeth. As you whistle a high note, raise the mid-portion of your tongue slightly by pushing it a little forward, as if you were saying "aah-eee, aah-eee." Push from the floor of your mouth, letting it rise and fall rapidly for a wavering effect. It requires practice, but the resulting vibrato adds a romantic dimension to your whistling.

TONGUE TIPPLING   ⊙ 38

Tongue Tippling is to Pucker Whistling what yodeling is to voice. By moving your tongue slightly, you can get an abrupt change in the pitch of your whistle, much like a whistled yodel. This is fairly advanced. Don't try this until you are fairly confident with your whistling ability.

For Tongue Tippling, the tongue is raised slightly off the floor of the mouth and eased back and forth.

Instead of whistling with your tongue against your bottom teeth, whistle a note with the tip of your tongue pulled back from your teeth, off the front floor of your mouth. While whistling, delicately ease the tongue forward (keeping it above the floor of your mouth) until the tip touches the bottom lip, just above your lower teeth. Practice this. You should work toward a sudden break in pitch.

Tongue Tippling works by suddenly altering the resonating chamber of your mouth. When the tongue is held back and off the floor of the mouth, the resulting cavity under the tongue helps determine the pitch. When you suddenly seal off this cavity by touching your tongue against the inside of your bottom lip, you drastically alter the pitch-determining chamber of your mouth, producing the abrupt break in notes.

Use Tongue Tippling to imitate birds and to add baroque trills to your whistled songs. It is an elegant effect and well worth the effort.

INVISIBLE WHISTLE

The purpose of the Invisible Whistle is to harass. It is not particularly musical, but it *is* invisible. That one quality makes it useful for all sorts of sonic shenanigans.

INSTRUCTIONS

1. Place your tongue lightly on the roof of your slightly opened mouth, allowing the edges of your tongue to form a seal against the inside roof, just above your teeth. The tip of your tongue should touch the roof about ⅛ to ¼ of an inch behind your front teeth.

2. Draw back the *very tip* of your tongue just slightly from the roof of your mouth so that you make a small opening between the tongue and the roof. The sides of your tongue are still sealed against roof just above the gums.

With mouth slightly open and relaxed, others can't tell you're whistling.

3. Very gently, blow air over your tongue so that it escapes through the little hole you have just made. Adjust the tongue to subtly change the size and shape of the hole until you can hear a whistling sound.

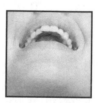

Tip of tongue drawn back slightly to form small hole on roof of mouth.

Be patient. The whistle will be faint at first. (Be sure your tongue is not squeezed—it must be placed ever so lightly on the roof.) You might try varying air pressure and raising and lowering your jaw slightly.

USES

This shrill little whistle is not loud, especially at first, but can be controlled to produce very nice music. With your mouth just barely open and a blank expression on your face, you can produce the whistle quite invisibly. In confined spaces such as automobiles, elevators, classrooms, and religious services, you will find this whistle to be good entertainment. Confused people will furrow their eyebrows. Thinking it's "the wind," they will open and close windows, adjust hearing-aid levels, and the like. Dogs are particularly put off by this. If you are clever enough to look serious, your whistle will go completely undetected. Subtle public harassment can be a fine and rewarding hobby—particularly if you are not caught.

Invisible Whistle SFX

There is an added feature of the Invisible Whistle. Because it is produced inside the mouth, you can use your lips to shape its sound for special effects. See Bird Tweets, Etc. (page 62), Touch Dialing (page 160), Moan-Back Beeps (page 143), and the Ice Cream Truck (page 142). For an endless whistle that will drive relatively sedate people around the bend, see the note on "Circular Breathing" in Chapter 6 (page 121).

2-FINGER WHISTLE

The art of hailing a taxi is the urban equivalent of lassoing a galloping horse. It takes determination, patience, and a lot of savvy to pull down a yellow cab. You may plant yourself in strategic positions and wave on tiptoe, but the Taxi Whistle is by far the safest and most effective device yet invented to halt a speeding hack.

There are two kinds of Taxi Whistles—those requiring the use of fingers, and those using only the mouth. Both will require patience and practice, but diligence will be royally rewarded with an ear-piercing shrill that will lock the brakes of cabs at two hundred yards.

INSTRUCTIONS

1. Open your mouth and draw your lower lip tautly inward to cover the top of your lower teeth.
2. Flattening your tongue, bring it forward to hover above the inside edge of your bottom lip.
3. Touch the tips of your little (pinkie) fingers together at the sides, at an angle of about 90 degrees.

4. Nails upward, insert the point of the fingertips, the V, just under the tip of your tongue, rolling the tip of your tongue upward and back a bit. Inside, the tongue tip is curved upward, toward—but not touching—the front roof of the mouth.

Tips of fingers inserted, tongue folded back, lower lip very taut.

5. Bring the upper lip down on the first joint of the pinkie fingers. Important: Look in the mirror. There should be a clean, triangular opening formed between the inside V of the fingers and the taut lower lip. (The key is a tight lower lip—it becomes the "edge of the bottle" you are blowing across.)

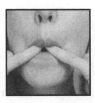

V-shaped hole formed between fingers and lower lip.

6. Blow briskly, directing air over the tongue and down across the triangular opening. (No air should escape from the corners of your mouth.)

7. Experiment. Adjust the tips of your little fingers, moving them just slightly apart. Vary their angles. Try various tongue tensions. Looking into a mirror can be a helpful way to monitor your adjustments.

Be patient. It will take a few sessions. Listen for the faintest "grab" of a whistle and you'll be on the right track. With practice you will soon be belting out decibels of shrill sound with this, the loudest method of whistling.

Dairy Products and Your Whistle

It is widely understood that a mouthful of soda crackers can put a damper on whistling. But what is not generally known is that dairy products—notably milk, cheese, and yogurt—are the scourge of good whistling. Before a performance, a serious whistler won't touch a glass of milk or a grilled cheese sandwich. Dairy products can alter the saliva-and-mucus balance in the mouth and throat to make whistling, and even singing, difficult (chiefly because many people as adults have slight to significant dairy allergies).

This is not to say you should avoid dairy products in general, but when you are backstage at the local talent show, about to make your whistling debut with "Shenandoah," you might give that milkshake a miss.

FINGERLESS WHISTLE

1 2 **3** **4**

40

The Fingerless Whistle is not an easy whistle to master. It demands practice and patient experimentation, but once captured, it is the most convenient of loud whistles.

INSTRUCTIONS

1. Open your mouth and draw your lower lip tautly inward to cover the top edge of your lower teeth.

2. Flattening your tongue, bring it forward to seal against the inside edge of your lower lip. Make your tongue slightly V-shaped, lifting the sides up a bit as you draw back the very tip of your tongue so that you create a small hole between the tongue tip and the middle-inside edge of your lower lip.

The resulting small hole between the lip and front of the tongue is critical. To form the hole properly, you must arch the tongue a little off the floor of the mouth as you draw back the tongue tip about ⅛ to ⅟₁₆ of an inch. (This is key—it forms the "bottle" or cavity you will be blowing across.)

3. Close your mouth slightly. Keep your upper lip pulled high, out of the way, and your lower lip tensed and taut.

4. Blow fairly gently, directing air over the hole by adjusting the channel—the slight V—of your tongue. As you blow, you will have to increase the tension of both lips. Do not blow too hard at first. Make small adjustments and listen for the slightest "grab" of a whistle.

The lower lip is very tightly drawn over the lower teeth, with the tongue lifted slightly off the floor of the mouth.

The tongue is sealed against a tight lower lip with the tip withdrawn to form a hole.

Because the Fingerless Whistle does not require the use of hands, it makes an excellent warning signal for use when skating, bicycling, skateboarding, skiing, and the like.

This whistle can also be used for all sorts of imitations with the use of cupped hands: such as birds (see the Seagull, page 82) and sirens. And, when combined with a hum: the Loon (page 79), Spinning Tires (page 136), the Blow-Dryer (page 158), and whining machinery.

Taxi Whistles

Unlike the Pucker Whistle, which uses the "whole tone effect," Taxi Whistles and Hand Coos (page 98) are produced by the physics principle of "edge tone," in which a rapidly moving stream of air rushes across an opening. The rush of air is directed at the edge of the opening in such a way that it sets up swirling eddies of air that disturb the airflow and generate whistling vibrations.

When we blow in a particular way across the opening of an empty bottle, this edge tone produces a low, steamshiplike whistle. Flutes, recorders, pipe organs, and even police whistles operate on this principle of splitting a rushing airstream into swirls of air to make sound vibrations.

For the Fingerless Whistle, you hold your tongue and lips so that a cavity forms under the tongue, and a small hole is formed between the tip of the tongue and lower lip. As you channel rushing air across the hole with your tongue, you get a powerful edge tone—and a loud whistle.

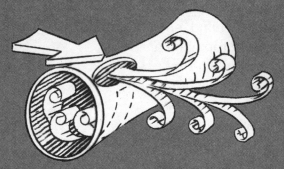

Air flow over flute opening

In the case of the Hand Coo, cup your hands to allow a hole to form between your thumbs. Inside is the cavity formed by your cupped hands. As you blow obliquely across the thumb hole you get the whistling coo. By changing the shape of the cavity, you can alter the resonating body of air to raise and lower pitch.

HAND COO

The sound of the Hand Coo is a cross between the woody softness of a recorder and the mellow ring of a dove. It has a gentle musical tone—a sound that will expand your whistle repertoire.

INSTRUCTIONS

1. Hold your opened hands, palms up, in front of you. Place one hand on top of the other, positioning the hands to overlap at right angles as in illustration A.

2. With the thumb and index finger of the bottom hand, encircle the fingers of the top hand at approximately the first knuckle, as in illustration B.

3. Rotate the hand just encircled 90 degrees toward you. The fingers should rotate within the thumb and index finger of the other hand, as in illustration C.

4. Allow the hand you just rotated to bend at the knuckles so that you can bring the thumbs of each hand together facing you. Adjust your hands so that they are comfortable, with an enclosed cavity inside the cup of your hands. Work at this until the hands seal this cavity completely.

The only air space should be the hole between your thumbs, as in illustration D.

5. Bend the thumbs at the top knuckle. (The thumbs should be symmetrical.) Place your upper lip at the bottom of your thumbnails, cover the knuckles with your slightly opened mouth, and blow gently, down *across* the hole between your thumbs, as in illustration E. Do not blow *into* the hole, but *across* it. (Again, it is just like blowing across the lip of a bottle.)

If the cavity is sealed and you are blowing across the hole formed by your thumbs, a cooing sound should blow forth. If not, try adjusting your hands. Pull them apart, shake them, and retrace the steps. Try different angles and speeds of blowing across the knuckle on your thumbs. With practice, your coo will come.

USES

Once you can produce a fairly strong, consistent "coo," let the middle, ring, and little fingers of the outside hand flap out at the bottom knuckles to change the pitch of your Hand Coo. With a little work, you can control this finger-flap to the point of playing songs. You will find that subtle changes with hand shape and speed of blowing can create new notes.

A. Hands overlapped at right angles.

B. Thumb and index finger encircle fingers of other hand.

C. Rotate the hand in encircled fingers 90 degrees so that thumb points up.

D. Bend hand to place thumbs symmetrically together. Be sure there is an enclosed hollow within hands.

E. Place your upper lip on your thumbnails and blow down across the hole between your thumbs.

HAND COO SIGNAL

The classic Native American ambush of cowboys was always preceded by Hand Coos—at least according to the Westerns on late-night cable. You, too, can use this classic stealth signal in the office, the classroom, the library, or at a singles mixer.

to signal inconspicuously across the room messages, such as "Check out the babe by the punch bowl," or "The good stuff's in the back."

INSTRUCTIONS

1. Use the finger-flap described for the Hand Coos to change the pitch of your coo rapidly.
2. Then trill your tongue (like a Spanish "r" sound) as you produce the Hand Coo.

USES

In the school library, Hand Coo Signals can be utilized to warn "Teacher's coming—get off the desk!" or at work, "The Boss is coming—get off the desk!" If you're caught cooing loudly, explain that you're just examining literature and demonstrating a passage from *The Last of the Mohicans* for your school or cubicle mates.

Similarly, Hand Coos make fine signals at crowded parties. You can prearrange the meanings of various Hand Coo Signals with a friend or partner. Then use the Hand Coo

Whistling Wind ⦿ 44

Wind is one of those evocative sound effects that sets the stage in a good story. In the old days of radio drama and film, wind was created by hand-cranking a rotating ribbed cylinder under a weighted square of heavy canvas. Whoever figured that out was a sound genius. You, however, don't have to be.

To feel the godlike rush of creating your own wind (so to speak), arch your tongue up in the back of your mouth, as if you are saying the sound of a "k." Without speaking, blow air out gently and listen for the "disturbance" of the air. Work towards a little hint of a whistle and you'll have it. You can change the sound of your wind—from balmy breeze to hurricane gales—by changing the shape of your mouth and tongue, like "khaaaa-oooo-aaaa-ohhhh." Let the wind swell and flow. You can even make it continuous by exhaling and then *inhaling* air, without a break.

The sound of wind is just the thing to set the atmosphere for a story . . . khaa-oooo . . . "It was a dark and stormy night. . . ."

DOUBLE WHISTLE

The Double Whistle is an amazing effect. By whistling out of the corners of your mouth, you can actually produce two whistle tones that can be used for harmonies or eerie effects. (But be forewarned: On the difficulty scale of one to four, this ranks a five. It probably takes more work to get than any other sound in the book.)

INSTRUCTIONS

1. Open your mouth slightly, point your tongue, and poke it out just through your lips. Keep your tongue somewhat stiff, and form two small (⅛-inch) holes at the corners of your mouth.

2. Blow very softly, adjusting your lips and tongue until you can hear a bit of a whistle. Focus first on getting the slightest hint of a whistle from one side. Finding that first one is the hardest, but once you get it, the second side will follow quickly. This will, no doubt, take a few sessions over a few days, but keep trying. Practice no more than a couple of minutes each time. With diligence and experimentation, you will be able to produce a whistle from each side of your mouth simultaneously.

Blow gently through two holes formed on either side of your slightly pointed tongue.

USES

You can use the Double Whistle for harmony on songs. Try "It's Crying Time Again," or "Dance of the Sugar Plum Fairies" from Tchaikovsky's *Nutcracker Suite.* It will amaze people.

The Double Whistle can be used for creepy theremin space effects as well. It has such a strange sound that it is almost impossible for your basic nearsighted office supervisor or teacher to locate. (It sounds as if a window is open somewhere or the steam heat is acting up.) Several fine high school teachers, in fact, have been driven to early retirement with skilled use of the Double Whistle.

NOSE WHISTLE

The Nose Whistle, or Nose Flute, is a little device made of wood, metal, plastic or pottery that sounds much like a little flute or ocarina—only you play it with your nose. You blow air from your nose through the Nose Whistle, and use your slightly open mouth as a resonant cavity to make a variety of sounds, from bird calls to sweet music.

The Nose Whistle has been found in many cultures, the earliest of which reportedly dates back to the Neolithic Era some 3000 years B.C. Various tribes in Polynesia and Indonesia reputedly believed that air from the nose contained the soul and thus was more spiritually and musically powerful. You can try it out and see for yourself.

The Nose Whistle is the only Mouth Sound in the book that uses a device—a device that you can make yourself from any good quality card stock or heavy stock paper and a couple of pieces of Scotch tape. See the page at the back of the book for two complete Nose Whistle patterns to cut, assemble, and play. Why two? An extra, as a spare or for duets.

INSTRUCTIONS

I–2.

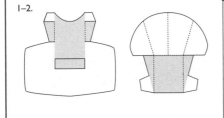

3.

1. Cut or tear out the Nose Whistle Pattern at the back of the book along the perforated edge.

2. The Nose Whistle pattern consists of two pieces: the "fipple base" and the "air guide," as shown. Cut carefully around the outside of each pattern.

3. In the center of the fipple base is the rectangular hole for the fipple hole itself. (Fipple, by the way, is an actual word for the hole of a whistle or flute over which air is blown.) Cut out the fipple hole especially carefully, leaving a straight, clean edge, or your whistle will not work well. Ideally, this cut should be done with a sharp art knife (an X-Acto knife or single-edge razor blade), but only with adult supervision and not under the influence of drugs or alcohol. (Stupid to actually have to write about it, but it makes my lawyers frisky.)

4. Cut along the short, red, solid lines, as indicated on both the fipple base and the air guide.

5. Carefully fold up sides C and D of both pieces along the red dotted lines, in the direction indicated by the arrows. (For precise folds, use a ruler or straightedge and first score the red dotted lines with a ballpoint pen. The resulting crease will allow you to make your folds crisper.)

6. Turn the air guide over and place it onto the face of the fipple base so that tab A and tab B on the air guide match up with A and B on the fipple base. Tabs C and D on the fipple base should match up with the back of tabs C and D on the air guide. The shaded area on each part will become the inside of the area you will blow through.

7. Make sure that the front edge of tabs A and B on the air guide are lined up exactly with the edge of the fipple hole of the fipple base. Use two small pieces of Scotch tape to attach air guide tabs A and B to the fipple base.

8. Use an additional two pieces of Scotch tape to attach fipple base tabs C and D to air guide tabs C and D (as matched up in step 6).

9. Look at the diagrams to check your work, and gently crease along the dotted lines of the rounded nose cover at the top of the air guide.

10. Finally, bend the fipple base slightly so that it barely arches to match the curve of your mouth.

HOW TO PLAY YOUR PAPER NOSE WHISTLE

1. Hold the Nose Whistle gently at its center (along the air guide), between your index finger and thumb. Shape your mouth as if you're making an "o" sound.

2. Press the Nose Whistle under your nostrils and flat against your open mouth. (You're going to look like a fool. Get over it.) The fipple hole should be centered over your open mouth.

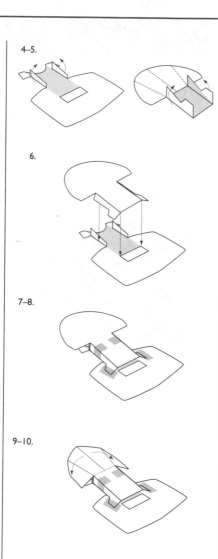

4–5.

6.

7–8.

9–10.

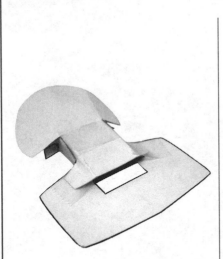

3. Arch your tongue against the back roof of your mouth, closing off your throat. Now, this is the odd-sensation part: Blow only through your nostrils, into the top of the air guide. That's right. Blow gently through your nose. With just a few adjustments, you should begin to hear a slight flute tone.

Experiment. Try blowing slightly harder or softer. Drop your tongue down inside your mouth so that your mouth cavity enlarges. Check to be sure there are no leaks at the corners of your mouth. It is key that the air guide directs your breath so that it blows across the fipple hole, hitting its outer edge. Try gently arching the base more or less so that it curves better over your mouth. Or, try adjusting the bottom of the fipple hole to catch the air better. In a matter of moments you'll move from vague tones to cleaner, louder notes. (See The Ploit, page 24 for tips on mouth resonance.)

USES

You'll rapidly discover that you can play strong, beautiful notes and songs. You can add vibrato to notes or make yodeling sounds by fluttering your tongue up and down. You can even play notes and hum at the same time—most excellent for psychedelic songs like "In-A-Gadda-Da-Vida." After ten to fifteen minutes of practice, most people can play just about any song imaginable.

Professional-sounding, slide-whistle sound effects can be created as well. Simply glide slowly from high note to low note and you have a plummeting coyote; glide upward from low to high and you have Jack's beanstalk or Pinocchio's nose growing.

If you play guitar, piano, or accordion and can accompany yourself, why not Scotch tape the paper Nose Whistle to your face to play the melody? It's a decidedly original and impressive talent for any beauty pageant contestant. Use a second Nose Whistle for duets, or make many more and start a Nose Whistle choir at the school or office. Suddenly a whole new world of musical novelty is open to you.

C H A P T E R 6

MUSICAL INSTRUMENTS

Music comes naturally to us. Even before humans articulated words, our apelike ancestors pounded on logs to produce primitive rhythms. In time, the voice developed, and we began to sing. Inspired, we invented all manner of percussion, stringed, and wind instruments to extend and accompany the music of the voice. Still, after centuries of evolution, no musical instrument can match the range, flexibility, and expressiveness of the human voice.

THE VIOLIN

More than any other instrument, the violin conjures up tradition and mystique. Maybe that's because playing a violin string is like playing a vocal cord. But don't let that bother you. Somewhere inside that dental work of yours lies a Stradivarius.

INSTRUCTIONS

1. Hold your lips nearly together, and slightly draw in your lower lip to rest your upper teeth on it.
2. With your finest falsetto, hum a high note. Project the note up and out through the small opening between your teeth and lower lip.

Teeth on lower lip to sharpen falsetto whine.

3. Vibrato (page 91), that beautiful wavering of pitch and volume, takes some practice, but is well worth the effort. It is essential for good mouth violin. Push air upward from your stomach muscles and diaphragm and blow out so that it pulsates through your mouth.

USES

The mouth violin is definitely a class act. As you produce the violin sound, cradle an imaginary violin under your chin with arm extended, and bow the invisible instrument with

The Mello Cello

44

The human voice can sound remarkably like a bowed cello. Using the mouth violin as your guide, hum low and slow in your best deep, baritone voice through slightly closed lips. Imagine languidly bowing the strings of a cello as you hum. Add vibrato for effect and try Beethoven's "Ode to Joy" or a slow, mournful rendition of "Gilligan's Island."

your other hand as you sway elegantly from side to side. Be suave. Be ever so delicate. Use the mouth violin to serenade the love of your life over a fine meal of fast food, soft drink, and fries or, if you are more intrepid, at a fine restaurant.

VIOLIN PIZZICATO

The violin is not always bowed to produce a singing tone. Sometimes the strings are lightly plucked to make soft, percussive sounds. This effect is called *violin pizzicato*.

From classical symphonies to elevator music, the pizzicato dances softly in the background of many major musical works. It was not until fairly recently, however, that the art of violin pizzicato reached its zenith in Carl Stalling's *Looney Tunes* orchestrations (for Daffy Duck's footsteps—as Daffy sneaks across the silver screen).

INSTRUCTIONS

1. Produce a high falsetto tone as you say the syllable "ta." Emphasize the burst of the "t."

2. Now put your lips together so that your bottom lip protrudes slightly. Continue saying your short "t" in a falsetto. The percussion of each "t" should vibrate your bottom lip sharply to form the pluck of your pizzicato. Practice until you get a single, sharp "pluck" of your lip with each note.

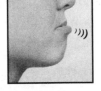

The lower lip vibrates with each note.

3. Slowly practice the musical scale. Then try faster scales and strains from any classical music that comes to mind. Start with "Yankee Doodle," move on to the "The Flintstones" theme, and then maybe Grieg's "Hall of the Mountain King" (en masse, and you will sound like the Boston Symphony). For best effect your violin pizzicato should be a rapid sequence of cascading notes.

USES

Try out your pizzicato on a Daffy Duck tiptoe sequence. Bend your elbows so that your arms are held in close (like a T-Rex) at chest level. Let your wrists go limp. Bend over slightly and produce your pizzicato scale as you stealthily tiptoe your way across the room —a perfect Saturday-morning cartoon sneak.

MOUTH MANDOLIN

Venice. Naples. Rome. All these can be yours with the Mouth Mandolin. There is nothing quite like the mandolin to conjure up images of the Old Country—canals, cappuccino, and overweight people stuffed into Gucci shoes. It's powerful stuff: The Mouth Mandolin and a red-checkered tablecloth are all you need to set a romantic mood for that certain someone.

INSTRUCTIONS

1. Tuck in your lips and pull them taut so that your mouth covers your teeth. Do not close your mouth, but keep your lips fairly close together. (If you look in the mirror, you will look like you are doing a pathetic imitation of a toothless old gondolier.)

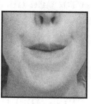

Lips are drawn in over the teeth.

2. In your finest Falsetto (page 23), sing a high, slightly nasal clear tone and hold it.

3. While singing the tone, take the tip of your tongue and rapidly brush it up and down across your in-turned lips. This fluttering will break your falsetto tone into the beautifully rapid vibration of a mandolin.

The tongue flutters up and down across the lips.

Your tongue-fluttering may be slow at first, but a little practice will give you the speed needed.

USES

Try "Santa Lucia" or other such Mediterranean hits on your Mouth Mandolin. Italians will fight just to inhale next to you. The tone of your mandolin will no doubt be improved after a few glasses of Chianti.

CLASSICAL GUITAR

The classical guitar is an acoustic guitar played in a concert hall by a long-fingered musician in a black tie. The classical mouth guitar, on the other hand, is merely a mouth played by a non-musician, usually while soaking in the bathtub. The sounds and enjoyment are the same. Only the methods and whereabouts differ.

INSTRUCTIONS

1. Follow the instructions for the Violin Pizzicato (page 109). The plucking sound of the lip vibration is similar.

2. In the Classical Guitar, however, the lip vibration is minimized and the normal tone is emphasized to produce a fuller, more robust sound.

The lower lip vibrates with each hummed note.

USES

Try musical scales and then graduate on to any slow, classical music such as Mozart's "Minuet in G," Bach's "Air on a G-string," or a stripped down version of Beethoven's Ninth Symphony. If these are unfamiliar, try "Farmer in the Dell."

ELECTRIC GUITAR

The electric guitar is just a violin with a V-8 engine. To coax the rubbery wails of an electric guitar out of your own mouth, all you have to do is wear tight jeans and imitate a violin (see Violin, page 108). Close your eyes, imagine a wall of amps behind you, and say "Bye-bye, frontal lobes." This creates the proper frame of mind.

INSTRUCTIONS

1. Hold your lips together, but slightly draw in your lower lip to allow your upper teeth to rest on it.

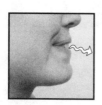

Teeth on the lower lip sharpen the falsetto whine.

2. Use a high, whining falsetto. Concentrate on projecting the whine up and out through the small opening between your teeth and lower lip. Adjust your lips and mouth until you make a sharp guitarlike tone.

3. Push air upward from your stomach and diaphragm to produce the wavering swells of a guitar tone by rhythmically varying the pressure. Vibrato in a guitar, as with a violin, is quite important.

The Fuzz 'n' Funk Bass Guitar

⊙ 46

Fuzz 'n' Funk Bass is a sweet effect—in the rock and soul sense. To do this, you do the bottom-lip buzz and the deep hum of the Tugboat Blast (see page 44). Stiffen your bottom lip and blow harder to raise the pitch; loosen your lip and blow more lightly to lower the notes. You will feel the pitch change quickly and begin to buzz out bass lines. For musicality, match your throat hum to the same note as your deep lip buzz. When you first simultaneously hit the same note with your hum and your lip buzz, you will feel a heady rush as the sounds reinforce each other. Wicked cool. With some practice, you can actually do killer wall-of-sound bass licks, à la Led Zeppelin ("A Whole Lotta Love"), Sly and the Family Stone riffs, or the ever-funky "Theme from *Shaft*." Shut yo' mouth.

Practice different tones and favorite guitar riffs, until you're not sure if that's you or B. B. King.

USES

Air Guitar, man! Everyone has at least one friend who is a holdover from Woodstock or, failing that, a holdout for Metallica. Whenever that person hears acid guitar yowls, he will suddenly screw his face into a pained expression and instinctively begin fretting an imaginary Fender Telecaster guitar. Those jerky contortions are called "getting into your axe." You must adopt this body language for your own mouth guitar imitations.

The mouth guitar can be used in combination with the Jazz Bass (see page 114), Drums (page 124), or the Human Beat Box (page 127) for some fine combo work. Remember to say *man* at the end of each sentence and sprinkle sentences with words like *heavy* and *gig*, and *know what I'm sayin'?*

Now, step aside and, 'scuse me while I kiss the sky . . .

THE JAZZ BASS

The bass is by far the most sensuous and shapely of musical instruments. Every night, with eyes half-closed, delicate-fingered players coax out its low, rich tones in smoky jazz clubs everywhere—stroking, plucking, slapping, bowing, or otherwise caressing the bass into thumps and moans.

INSTRUCTIONS

1. With a soft, low tone, sing the sounds "duh, duh, duh."

2. Put your lips together so that your bottom lip protrudes slightly, as if you were pouting. Continue saying your low "duh's." The bottom lip should be slightly tensed so that it is blown out a little with the percussion of each "duh." Practice until you get a single, sharp "pluck" of your lip with each note.

Each hummed note blows out the lower lip a little bit.

3. Work on a musical scale. Keep your "duh's" low, humlike, and very resonant, just like a bass. As you feel more comfortable with your mouth bass, try plucking your way slowly and sensuously through such songs as "Misty," "Breaking Up Is Hard to Do," "It Had to Be You," or jazz standards such as "Satin Doll." Playing along with your favorite CD is excellent practice.

USES

To play a really mean mouth bass, you must close your glassy eyes at least three-quarters. Roll your head back dreamily and mime-fret the neck of an imaginary bass with one hand while plucking "strings" with the fingertips of the other. Lay back. Be cool—*verrry* cool.

THROAT BAGPIPES

Bagpipes really need a couple of droning tones along with that nasally whine of the lead pipe, or chanter. But you can perform a solo chanter that simulates the effect quite well.

Drones

◉ 49

Whenever you happen upon a good droning sound, from the electronic hum of keys in the ignition to an offensively loud fan or the whine of a coffee grinder, it's your chance to shine—try bagpiping or Gregorian chanting over it. In a high, falsetto voice, chant in your best "Latin": "Hmmmmm . . . my father plays dominoes better than your father plays dom-in-oes . . . in excesses dai-ly . . ."

INSTRUCTIONS

1. Make a mega-nasal whine, by humming a harsh "eeee" sound, kicking it high into your nasal mask. Hum something like "Amazing Grace."

2. At the beginning of each note, gently hit the side of your Adam's apple with your stiffened fingers, so you get a little squeak on each note. There's your bagpipe chanter lead. (Don't overdo the little throat hit or you'll be doing your bagpiping in a doctor's waiting room.)

USES

Try getting a couple of people to each hum a low note, then do your bagpipe above them—you'll be 'avin' a right Scottish time, you will.

115

THE TRUMPET

The trumpet is really a New Year's Eve noisemaker that got out of control—the instrument most to blame for half-time marching-band versions of "Star Wars," "Never on a Sunday" and "Climb Ev'ry Mountain." Its tones can vary from a slow, silken softness to the grinding razz of a strip club.

INSTRUCTIONS

1. With a moderately high falsetto, make a single, nasal tone. To keep this tone nasal-sounding, raise the back of your tongue slightly, as if to say an "a" as pronounced in the word *back*.

2. Now use this nasal-esque sound to sing "taa-taa-taa" in a high falsetto voice a few times. Keep thinking of a trumpet sound—its quality and tone.

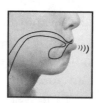

An arched tongue adds nasal quality.

3. Once you are comfortable with your "taa-taas," put your lips together, allowing your bottom lip to protrude slightly, with just a little tension.

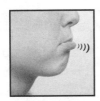

The lower lip vibrates with each note.

4. As you sing your "taa-taa's," emphasize the "t" of the "taa's" so that each "taa" is breathy enough to blow out and vibrate your bottom lip slightly. Work at this until you have just the slightest touch of lip vibration with each note. (It may be easier to add this lip vibration from the side of your mouth.) Practice on such trumpet standards as "Taps," "Reveille," or a John Philip Sousa march.

USES

Your trumpet provides excellent embellishment to radio music, and sounds particularly wonderful solo, in the concert hall of your bathroom. Try your own arrangements of such standards as "Misty," "Girl from Ipanema," Titanic's "My Heart Will Go On," or Justin Timberlake's "Cry Me A River." Delight your friends or fellow office workers by creating your own Muzak in elevators, or gather a few colleagues, teach them the trumpet, and form a brass ensemble for the next office bash.

Any mouth trumpet player worth a toot must wear an expression of concentration on his face. Place the thumb of your trumpet-valve hand just below your mouth and use your three fingers to press imaginary trumpet valves. For those dazzling high notes, be sure to throw your head back, arch your back, and act as if you are in great pain. This gives the impression you have soul.

Radio and Old 78s

⊙ 51

To do the sound of an old 78 r.p.m. record, hold your nose as in the Muted Trumpet to give yourself a nasal sound. First, do the needle drop with a little static (a crunchy "keeeee" sound), followed quickly by a rhythmic "shook-ahhh, shook-ahhh, shook-ahhh," then proceed with a muted trumpet number. Singing in a nasal voice sounds oh-so-grand. If you want to keep the crackle of radio or 78 records underneath you, just crackle cellophane rhythmically in your hand.

THE MUTED TRUMPET

The muted trumpet recalls the bygone era of big bands, fox-trots, and huge maroon cars with bulbous fenders. Create your own brand of nostalgia with the Muted Mouth Trumpet.

INSTRUCTIONS

1. Sing the same nasal "taa-taa's" you did for the regular mouth trumpet.

2. With the base of the thumb and the base of the index finger of one hand, gently pinch your nostrils closed. The palm of your hand should cover your mouth and will act as your trumpet mute.

3. As you sing your very nasal "taa-taa's," open and close your cupped hand over your mouth to achieve the "waa-waa" sound of the mute.

Pinch nostrils closed to mute mouth with hand.

USES

Practice on a few songs such as "It Had to Be You," "You Made Me Love You," and "Auld Lang Syne," but any old tune worth remembering is worth trying. Have several open-minded friends play their muted mouth trumpets and form a virtual big-band orchestra.

For other sound effects that use this Muted Trumpet, see "Radio and Old 78s" on page 117, and "Phone Voice" (page 163).

THE FRENCH HORN

T he French horn is an instrument that sounds as if it is coming from the next room even when it is being played right in front of you. Like a distant sound, the French horn naturally has a muted softness to it. And your imitation of the instrument will reflect this.

INSTRUCTIONS

1. With a moderately high, nasal falsetto, sing the words "boh, boh, boh" in an ascending musical scale. Practice this a few times.

2. Now place your lips together in a relaxed and loose manner.

3. Sing your "boh's," with an especially strong nasal quality. Close your lips at the start of each note so that your cheeks push out with air and then collapse with each "boh," as the lips are pushed apart and air escapes. You must work toward just a touch of loose lip vibration with each note.

The cheeks billow out loosely with each note.

USES

It's possible to create a nearly flawless imitation of an English hunting horn with your mouth French horn.

A hunting horn makes a fine wake-up call when directed into the ear of a loved one and is guaranteed to roust even the most comatose sleeper.

THE TROMBONE

Although many songs of the big-band era had wonderful trombone solos, the trombone is now mostly relegated to brassy backup work. A metallic blast of a trombone does, however, have the rather special ability to grab a melody and catapult it to the top row of any bleacher. In fact, a good Saturday-afternoon, halftime trombone section can deafen and even kill at close range.

Your mouth trombone may not have the raw power of the real thing, but it will have every bit of its flexibility.

The One-Man Trombone Band

⊙ 53

Try doing your brassiest mouth trombone in a marching-band number, say, "Stars and Stripes Forever." Stomp your feet on the downbeats as you march around and, at the same time, clap your hands on the offbeats. It almost sounds as noisy as a real band. No doubt, friends and family will either join the parade . . . or ask you to march in the street.

INSTRUCTIONS

Follow the directions for the Trumpet (page 116), but instead of making "taa-taa's" in a high falsetto, produce low-pitched, deep, nasal "taa-taa's." The lip vibrations will be identical.

The lower lip vibrates with each note.

USES

The Trombone can be used to play any marching-band classic, from the ever-patriotic John Philip Sousa's "Stars and Stripes Forever" to the ever-festive "Seventy-Six Trombones."

The mouth trombone is a natural for large numbers at a party. Guests can form lines and razz their way through intricate marching-band formations in your living room. You might try a halftime favorite such as a "A Marching Salute to the American Automobile." Several people arrange themselves to form the outline of a car while a few others rotate round-and-round as wheels—all to the tune of "In My Merry Oldsmobile."

Circular Breathing

Circular breathing is a fascinating vocal technique used by players of wind and brass instruments from oboes to trumpets to (most notably) didgeridoos. Relied upon by professional musicians, it's a technique you might find useful for holding a note or a MouthSound without pausing to breathe.

It's impossible to breathe in and blow out at the same time, but it is possible to maintain air pressure *without blowing from your lungs.* Try puffing your cheeks with air, holding it, and breathing independently through your nose. This is the principle you use to breathe circularly—disengaging your *breathing* from your *blowing.*

You use your mouth and cheeks like the airbag of a bagpipe, building a reservoir of air that maintains the drone. Maintaining pressure, you ease the air out of your cheeks for a moment (using cheek muscles only) as you sniff in a quick breath through your nose, thereby topping up your lungs without stopping your blowing.

Try this with a particularly high Invisible Whistle (page 92, ⊙ 39) or the Fly Buzz (page 68). You can drive teachers, lecturers—anyone—crazy with a high-pitched whistle or little buzz that never stops. Drivers in a car are convinced "a window is open somewhere."

THE SAXOPHONE

Peppered with all sorts of valves and hatches, the saxophone resembles some weird, galactic space colony. But the sax is really a very down-to-earth instrument with tremendous range: It can have a mellow fullness unmatched by any other musical instrument, or the gravel-voiced nastiness of the gutter.

INSTRUCTIONS

1. Imitation of the saxophone requires a special hollow resonance of the mouth. Open your mouth partway and draw in your bottom lip tautly over your bottom teeth.
2. Seal the front edge of your tongue against your bottom lip, arching the back of your tongue up to allow a hollow cavity to form under your tongue. The back of the tongue should almost touch the roof of the mouth.

The front edge of the tongue seals against the tucked lower lip.

3. In a comfortable, mid-range voice, sing a soft "a" sound. (The "a" should be nasal, as in the word *back.*) Experiment with your lip and arched tongue until you hear a hollow, breathy quality in the tone.
4. Practice a musical scale and work on your breath control.

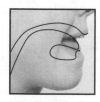

The tongue is arched off the floor of the mouth.

USES

The mouth sax can be a dead ringer for the real thing. Use vibrato and a sort of throaty breathiness to add realism. Try a soft falsetto, too. This will produce a sound much like the tone of a tenor saxophone. Slow, moody songs like "I've Grown Accustomed to Her Face," "Feelings," "Moon River," and "Yesterday" make perfect dentist office–type sax numbers. With two friends, one on Brushes (page 126) and another on the Bass (page 114), you can have some dynamite jazz jams.

Down and Dirty  54

Dirty sax is that sassy, razzy, jazzy sax with a nasty bite. It is the saxophone of 1950s rock 'n' roll and hot jazz. To make a dirty mouth sax, shape your mouth as in a normal Saxophone, but instead of singing a mellow tone, let your voice explode with a low, harsh, and gravelly "a" (as in back) sound. The sounds should issue forth with a grungy, gruntlike quality.

THE DRUMS

Yeah, man . . . For your MouthSound repertoire, there are four basic percussion effects: the snare drum, the bass drum, the cymbals, and the brushes.

INSTRUCTIONS

BASS OR KICK DRUM   ⊙ 55

Close your mouth. Say a "buh" sound. Now, as you say a "buh," let your cheeks puff slightly with air. Try this a few times. Then, simultaneously, add to this puffy-cheeked, explosive "buh" a touch of the Palate Grind (see page 25). This is the Bass Drum.

MARCHING SNARE   ⊙ 55

1. Produce the Palate Grind (page 25).
2. Practice the Palate Grind to make it sound like the roll of a snare drum. Starting with the back of the tongue raised against the palate (like a "guh" sound), abruptly and explosively make a series of bursting Palate Grinds. With the correct rhythm, these Palate Grinds can sound much like the drum cadence of a marching band. Now try alternating the Marching Snare with your Bass Drum.

Palate Grind produced in the back of the mouth for drums.

JAZZ SNARE 1   ⊙ 55

A second mouth snare technique is simply to exhale a strong "pff" sound. Do this a few times. Try alternating this Alternate/Jazz snare with your Bass Drum. BUH-pff . . . BUH-pff . . . BUH-pff . . . BUH-pff-pff . . .

JAZZ SNARE 2   ⊙ 55

A third mouth snare is similar, except you inhale a quick burst of air beginning with a "puh" sound. (Listen to the CD. It will help.) To learn this, first, try exhaling a "puh" sound; immediately, *inhale*

In Yo' Face: Rock 'n' Pop Rhythms

In popular music, the snare usually alternates with the bass or kick drum. The bass drum goes on the downbeats (ones and threes), like this: ONE, two, THREE, four. ONE, two, THREE, four.

The snare—and its sound can vary a great deal—is usually on the offbeats (the twos and fours), like this: one, TWO, three, FOUR. one, TWO, three, FOUR.

When you put them together, you have what's become the basic rock beat. They alternate with one another and drive the music. Be sure to listen on the CD.

the "puh" sound. Try doing the "puh" in and out quickly. The inhaled "puh" is your offbeat snare, particularly when alternated with your Bass Drum: BUH-puh, BUH-puh, BUH-puh, BUH-puh-puh.

If you make this Bass Drum hammer in a fast-driving beat with a strong "b" sound, you have Euro-disco sound. Add a Jazz Snare on the off beats.

TOM-TOMS ⊙55

After you become accomplished with your Snare Drum and Bass, you can add Tom-toms (deeper, throatier drums) by saying "dooo" in a deep voice.

CYMBAL 1 ⊙55

This cymbal is quite easy. Place your tongue tightly behind your clenched teeth. Allow a sizzling burst of air to push through your lips in a sort of "psss." Practice a beat, then hit the cymbal hard, letting the hissing sound fade slowly.

CYMBAL 2 ⊙55

For another type of cymbal—and to get air when you're doing a string of drum sounds—try putting your tongue tightly against your front teeth with your mouth closed. Then explosively pull in air through the corners of your mouth. Let it rush in past your tongue making a sort of "psssh" sound.

CIRCUS DRUM ROLL ⊙55

The Circus Drum Roll is a great MouthSound for the inveterate show-off. Produce your Snare Drum Roll, followed immediately by the clash of your mouth Cymbal. The roll can be used impressively to add pomp and ceremony to any act from knocking back a beer to tying your shoes. You can hold the rapt attention of an audience during even the most mundane task.

Or try the ol' Bump 'n' Grind. You can make a great Bump 'n' Grind—a kind of stripper vamp—that's useful for many occasions, especially when you want to be suggestive, or call attention to the passing hottie. It's a combo of Bass, Snare, and Cymbal. T-t-t-t-t, BUH-pff, BUH-BUH-pff, BUH-pff, BUH-BUH-PSSsssssss. Listen on the CD. Add a little Dirty Sax (page 123) and . . . oh, Mama . . .

BRUSHES ⊙55

For jazz buffs, no percussion section would be complete without the smoky sounds of the brushes. Rhythm and softness are important.

In a whispering breath of air, make the sound of "tchi, chu-chu, tchi, chu-chu, tchi" with soft emphasis on the "tchi's." You will have to hear it.

Use the brushes in a MouthSounds jazz combo, with the Bass and Sax or Trumpet. The Brushes can be combined in sequence with the Snare, Bass Drum, and Cymbal for a real jazz sound.

Human Beat Box 56

Over the past few years, rap music has gone to new places, in a sonic sense. Its crunched, fractured, splintered beats mixed with classic whiffs of riffs have completely broken open the traditional rhythm tracks of bass, drum, and snare. Anything goes, mouth sounds and all, as long as it hits a groove. This is great news for MouthSounders.

Perhaps best known of the many vocal percussionists is Rahzel, hip-hop's self-proclaimed "Godfather of Noyze." He blasted onto the urban music pavement as a member of the cutting-edge group, The Roots, where he pumped vocal sound effects into unbelievably acrobatic mouth percussion.

For your own vocal percussion, use all of the above sounds and rhythm effects, along with any other vocal effects in the book. Mix aggressive grunge and soft silk. Jam a plastic coffee cup over your mouth on regular off beats. Pop your percussive beat through a paper towel tube and such. Play around. Experiment.

On the CD are a few MouthSound Beat Box grooves—spacious down-tempo rhythms, up-tempo combinations, and sizzly stuff in between. Grab a few ideas and make them your own.

STEEL DRUMS

The steel drum—the happy, hollow metallic sound of Caribbean and calypso— was first made in the 1930s in Trinidad. Still hammered from 55-gallon oil drums, "the pans" have spread around the world and now . . . into your mouth.

INSTRUCTIONS

1. In a moderately high falsetto (see Falsetto, page 23) say a soft, hollow "boong," swallowing the "g" so that the sound rings with a nasal "nnnng." Do this a few times and begin singing notes. As you do this, try to kick the sound up into your nose, so that it rings in your nasal mask, and keep your cheeks very loose so that they billow out a touch at the beginning "buh" of each note.

2. On some notes, hold on to the drumming of the note by rapidly waggling your tongue just in and out of your mouth or by saying "muh" rapidly. Try varying your tones a touch by saying not only a lazy "boong," but "bong" and "bl-ongs." On paper, this might seem difficult, but listen to the CD and you will hear it.

USES

Try performing moderate-tempo ballads at first, like "Jamaica Farewell," "Marianne," or (a stretch), "Have You Seen the Muffin Man?" or "Goodbye, Ruby Tuesday." Make your songs swing with calypso beat, and most any song will do.

Get a few people to do this with you to form a Caribbean Mouth Steel Band. The next office party will never be the same. Guaranteed, mon.

Folk Mouth Instruments:
The Jaw Harp, Didgeridoo & Nose Flute

⊙ 59

Many ancient folk instruments, including various twangers and resonant tubes, use the mouth to create musical sounds. The **Jaw Harp**—also called the Jew's harp (most probably from the Old English

word for it, *gewgaw*)—is one of the most widespread. An ancient instrument, it is made from bamboo in Southeast Asia and metal in Africa and Europe. Often used to invoke a trance with its droning, harmonic sound, it is called *scacciapensieri* (or "thought-squasher") in Italian. The jaw harp is held to the mouth and strummed or plucked to play a fundamental

tone, and the mouth is able to shape and accentuate various harmonics. In America it is heard in jug bands and country and folk music. It is played by means of the Ploit Principle (see page 24).

The **Didgeridoo** is an instrument of Australia's Aboriginal

people that may date back 20,000 to 50,000 years. Players of the didgeridoo create deep, sonorous drones and rhythms by buzzing their lips. A true didgeridoo is a long tube, made naturally from a termite-hollowed eucalyptus tree, with a beeswax mouthpiece. Using a

technique known as "circular breathing" (see page 121), experts can keep the drones playing, without interruption, for hours. Didgeridoos, once very exotic and hard to hear, have become popularized in atmospheric movie soundtracks and dance music, and are now heard around the world.

Versions of the **Nose Whistle** have been around for about 5000 years. Once made of clay or wood, they are now quite popular in plastic. Or you can make one out of paper with instructions in this book (see page 103).

HAWAIIAN NOSE HUM

1 2 3 4 ◉

58

It has been said that the hum is God's gift to those who can't remember the words to songs. The Hawaiian Nose Hum represents one of the finest variations of this divine contribution. It's as fine as a nasal effect gets, especially when used in choruses and choirs.

INSTRUCTIONS

1. Keeping the mouth closed, press the tip of an index finger (or "Mr. Pointer," for four-year-olds and stoners) beside one nostril, closing it.

(*Note:* Do not *insert* index finger, as you may become the butt of cruel jokes.)
2. With a high falsetto voice, begin humming your favorite Hawaiian melody. Remember to keep your mouth closed. With your other index finger, stroke down gently on the open nostril, closing it momentarily, just as you begin each note of the tune. The result should be a mildly percussive, nasal guitar sound.

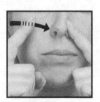

The index finger closes your open nostril with each note.

Develop your own style, using vibrato and hand flourishes. Don't be reticent to nose humming in the bathroom. Tile provides an especially fine echo effect. Showers and toilet flushes evoke tropical waterfalls.

USES

The Hawaiian Nose Hum can be particularly rewarding when accompanied by a ukulele or a harmonizing chorus of four or more. Of course, grass skirts are festive, as are pineapple punch and pupu platters.

You can also adopt the basic nose hum to simulate the pedal steel guitar of country and western songs. All you have to do is *think* Hank Williams to draw out those wailing swells of country music. The steel guitar nose hum lends a wonderful touch to late nights at a pancake house or roadside diner, or as an accompaniment to a honky-tonk jukebox.

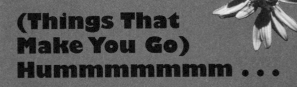

(Things That Make You Go) Hummmmmmm . . .

The word *hum* is an exquisite example of onomatopoeia—a word that is the sound itself. Where did it come from?

The old Dutch word for honeybee was *hommel,* a variation of which entered the English language around the fourteenth century, when the little whirring insect came to be called *humbylbee.* Eventually the name changed to the modern *bumblebee,* but the root word *hum,* the sound of the bumblebee, stayed with us.

CHAPTER 7

MISCELLANEOUS MOUTHSOUNDS

T his chapter dips into the hearty soup of sounds that perpetually surrounds us, offering some of the most notable. Transportation sounds, household noises, and space effects give the reader and would-be show-off spoonfuls of sounds to spice up storytelling, add conversational color, and grab attention.

THE CLUNKER

Old cars—those duct-taped contraptions with rusty bumpers, bent fenders, and coat hangers for antennae—ply the avenues and byways of America, spewing out smoke and all sorts of mechanical misfires. You now have an audio license to drive one.

INSTRUCTIONS

1. Purse your lips together and blow through them so that they flap loosely.

2. As you do, produce the Palate Grind (page 25). The combination makes a good stand-in for a rapidly rusting clunker, rumbling down the street.

Palate Grind is combined with a loose buzz of the lips.

3. To age the engine, move your tongue around inside your mouth as you do the above. Try pushing your tongue forward so that air rattles around it. This adds some quality, blue-smokin' misfires.

To add more personality to your '62 Buick, add a long, labored start on a cold morning by making a tired "Jaa-EE—Ah-ee—Ah-eeee . . ." When the engine turns over, add some tongue flaps, deep guttural grunts, and then crank 'er up. Add shifting gears and you're off! Well, sorta.

Zoom, Zoom, Zoom

In this age of mobility, we spend lots of time sitting quietly, slightly dazed, being transported from one spot to another. We may be behind the padded dash of a car, staring blankly on a train or plane, or on a crowded bus with a stranger's umbrella in our ribs. Sounds rush all around us. Subway doors bing-bong before swooshing shut. Gears grind, engines rev, brakes squeal. Helicopters and planes tear the air. These sights and sounds are an everyday part of our world.

The Doppler Effect ⊙60

You have just stepped off the curb and are about to cross the street against the light. Suddenly someone in a car speeding toward you sits on the horn—*whaaa!* You jump back. As the car races past, suddenly the sound of the car horn drops down a note—*whaaaa-oooooo!* In addition to scaring the crapola out of you, this little sonic event demonstrates the Doppler effect.

Christian Johann Doppler, a nineteenth-century Austrian physicist, first explained this phenomenon. As Doppler described it, sounds from an *approaching* object are higher pitched to a stationary listener than the same sounds from a *receding* object. As the sound source approaches, the sound waves become compressed and more vibrations strike the ear per unit of time (causing a sensation that is perceived as higher in pitch). As the sound source moves away, the sound waves become less condensed, causing an abrupt lowering of pitch.

When imitating moving objects such as speeding cars, abruptly lower the pitch of the sound to simulate the movement and this Doppler effect.

SPINNING TIRES

Stuck in the muck. The sound of tires spinning helplessly in the snow or mud is a good sound to have in the tool kit of your audio trunk.

INSTRUCTIONS

1. The Spinning Tire effect is just a Loon call (page 79) with a hum. So, start by making the Fingerless Whistle (page 96). That's the most difficult part.

2. Now hum as you continue to make the Fingerless Whistle. Let your pitch rise and fall. There you have some nice spinning sounds.

3. To put icing on the tires, so to speak, take your index or pointing finger, place it just

Move finger rapidly against chin.

below your lip, and, as you hum and whistle, shake your lip gently but rapidly up and down. You'll hear tires sinking in a snowbank or mud hole.

THE SPORTS CAR

The spritely, breezy buzz of little red sports cars will quicken the pulse of any sixteen-year-old . . . or sixty-year-old. Here are the keys.

INSTRUCTIONS

1. This is a two-part sound. To make the first part, push your lips out into a tight pucker, then blow through them to make a moderately high buzzing sound.

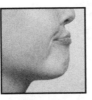

Blow through tightly puckered lips.

2. For the second part, trill your tongue on the front roof of your mouth just as though you were rolling your tongue for a Spanish or Scottish "r."

3. Produce both sounds together: the buzz of the pucker and the tongue trill.

Tongue flutter behind buzzing lips.

4. Experiment until you get this sports car–like sound.

USES

Using the Doppler Effect (page 135), you can imitate the sound of a speeding car passing by. Abruptly lower the pitch of the pucker-buzz as the car passes. Try simulating the Daytona 500 as cars of different sizes and speeds race past you.

SCREECH 'N' SKID

Making vocal skids and crashes is therapeutic. It dials back your memory to those salad days of crawling across the den floor to crash a toy car into Dad's foot—the starting block for a lot of sound makers.

INSTRUCTIONS

1. There's no shortcut to the Screech 'n' Skid. It has to be done like you're a six-year-old. First, load up with air, and hold your breath.

2. Now squeeze hard and let the sound squeak out in your highest falsetto voice. If it's rough and gravelly, so much the better. (If your face gets red and you pop a button, it's your own damn fault.) Let the screech rise and fall in pitch and volume.

USES

The Screech 'n' Skid is the perfect response when someone makes a profoundly dumb suggestion, asks an inane question, or proffers a *really* bad idea such as "Let's wash the cat" or "How 'bout a double for the road?" or "Why don't we bungee jump out of this hot-air balloon?" The Screech 'n' Skid is the ultimate reality check.

THE CRASH

This is the classic multi-purpose crash, good for all modes of transportation that come to an abrupt halt, the hard way.

INSTRUCTIONS

1. Load up air, and make your most explosive "buh," forcefully.
2. Add to this, simultaneously, a hard "kuh" on the roof of your mouth. (See Palate Grind, page 25.) It's not clear that this makes a significant sound out loud, but it adds a satisfying, deep vibration to the head, much like the rumble-pack option on a video game.

Practice a few times, and it will all come back to you. Let the crash explode out of your mouth,

singly or in series (depending on how big the fireball is), and finish it off with "Shhhhushes" and sizzling "S sounds."

USES

Introduce the Crash with the passing rev of the Sports Car (page 137) and the tire Screech 'n' Skid. As a lovely touch, wait a beat after the crash effect and add metallic debris hits in the form of little nasally "booonks," and a distant, rolling hubcap in the form of a soft "kuh" that you shape with your lips into a rhythmic rolling "kuh-ooo . . . wha-oo, wha-oo, wha-oo, wha-oo . . ." ◉63

SIRENS AND ALARMS

There are several different kinds of sirens, each of them making excellent warning alarms useful for child rearing and spousal discipline.

INSTRUCTIONS

THE SIREN WAIL ⊙63

1. The Siren Wail is the clean, old-fashioned siren. It is simply a high-falsetto wail, but muted a bit, with your teeth placed on your bottom lip. (Oddly enough, see Violin, page 108, for more details).

2. Push the sound hard and let it swell up and down slowly, trailing downward and off at the end. (For a similar sound, see the Submarine Dive Siren, page 148.)

Place top teeth on bottom lip to mute falsetto wail.

THE KLAXON BUZZER ⊙63

This is the aggressive, harsh, deep gravelly buzz of ambulances and alarms used in urban areas.

1. Do a Glottal Fry (page 26) by getting a big load of air in your lungs, holding your breath, and then pushing out air to make a long, grunting sound. (It actually uses the vibrations of your false vocal folds.)

2. Do this in succession, in the strongest, most explosive, and hardest-hitting manner you can stand. That's the Klaxon Buzzer—it all but screams "Get out of the way, you idiot!" It also sounds like it could be "Life's Penalty Buzzer."

Push air out in long, grinding grunt.

THE WHOO-WOO SIREN ⊙63

This is the sound of hospital ambulances behind you in mall traffic, and the neighbor's burglar alarm that triggers several times a week.

1. To make this part-siren, part-circus sound, simply say in a high falsetto voice, "WHAO-oo, WHAO-oo, WHAO-oo, WHAO-oo."

USES

For the sound of your neighbor's car alarm at 6:00 A.M., combine all the sirens into a lovely repeating medley of alarms, and include one more alarm: Shout "Move-away-from-the-car. Move-away-from-the-car . . ." in a deep, robotic, pro-wrestler kind of voice.

MOAN-BACK BEEPS ⊙64

To make the sound of large vehicles backing up, you need Moan-Back Beeps—the warning, back-up beeps that trucks and loaders yelp, as some guy standing behind them waves his hand and calls out to the driver, "Moan back . . . 'at's it . . . moan back . . ." (Author note: Yeah. OK. Old joke. Sorry.)

1. To make your own beeps, do the Invisible Whistle (page 92) in little bursts.

2. Begin each burst with lips together as if you were saying a "b" sound.

USES

This is an excellent sound to use when you back up and need room, or, more pointedly, when you happen to see a rather large family member backing away from the refrigerator. No words. Point made. Insult delivered.

THE ICE CREAM TRUCK

1 2 3 4

64

Ice cream trucks everywhere seem to have the same canned music blaring out of tinny bullhorn speakers. You can do your impression by adapting the Invisible Whistle (page 92).

INSTRUCTIONS

1. Begin each note with lips together as if you were saying a "b" sound, as described in Moan-Back Beeps (page 143).

2. Then simply whistle the irritating little melody—a little draggy and out of tune, like a bad tape loop. Watch as kids come running with quarters.

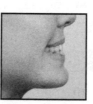

Lips pulled back as you do the Invisible Whistle.

THE FLYBY

All Flyby MouthSounds employ some form of the Palate Grind (page 25). But the use of the Doppler Effect (page 135) to infer movement will really make you an ace.

INSTRUCTIONS

THE CESSNA   ◉65

Use the Sports Car sound (page 137) with a long drawn-out Doppler Effect (page 135) for a perfect small-airplane-diving flyby.

THE JET   ◉65

1. Make the gravelly Palate Grind, and add to it a moderate to high-pitched hum. Your mouth should shape the sound into a sort of "oh."
2. Let this approaching jet sound build, then suddenly pass, by dropping in pitch (see the Doppler Effect, page 135) as you shift the sound forward in your mouth and shape it more into an "eeee" sound. (So the sound of your hum and the Palate Grind goes forward in your mouth, "Oooow-weeeeeeeeeee," and then fades.)

THE ROCKET   ◉65

For the swoosh of small rockets, begin with a gravelly "k" sound in the back of your mouth. Make it glide quickly forward and transition to a strong "whsssssssh" that trails off. This

should feel like—and sound a bit like—you are bringing up phlegm.

For larger rockets, cup your hands over your mouth and do a lower, slower version of the Jet Flyby.

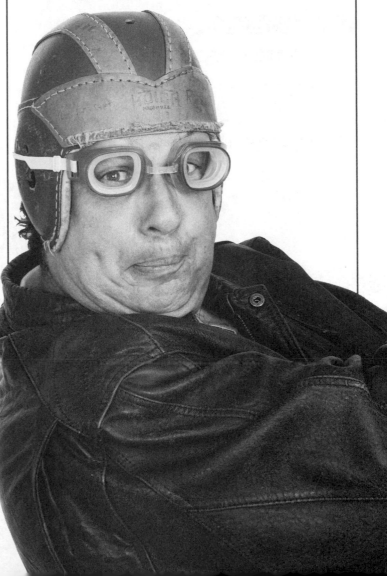

THE HELICOPTER

The helicopter is the human version of the bumblebee. Choppers, of course, don't make honey or pollinate flowers—but then, bees don't bring us live traffic reports in the morning. It all works out. Here's the spin.

INSTRUCTIONS

THE TAKEOFF ⊙65

1. Keep your lips gently closed. Place your tongue tip just barely through them, as if you were about to spit. But, instead of spitting (which involves pushing air out), quickly pull your tongue back and *suck in* air, so forcefully that it snaps your lips together. You should get a windy little pop—a chopping sound. Practice this.

2. Do this chopping sound repeatedly, increasing speed for the rotor takeoff. Pulling your tongue back and drawing in more air makes more wind, and the chopper will take flight.

3. Decreasing the wind and increasing the little chop will make the chopper fade into the distance. You may even be able to keep the distant chopper going by switching from *inhaling* the chops to *exhaling* them.

THE CHOPPER FLYBY ⊙65

Similar principle but different method. You can use the above for landings and takeoff, but this technique is a way to really increase the speed of a helicopter flyby.

1. Tuck your lips inward so that they cover the upper and lower teeth. (You'll look like a toothless old geezer about to down a bowl of oatmeal.)

Lips are drawn in over the teeth.

2. Close your mouth, allowing a small opening between your tucked lips.

3. Draw in air through the little opening as you rapidly run the tip of your tongue up and down across the inward-protruding edges of your lips to produce the "chopping" sound of the helicopter. For a fast Flyby, be sure to drop the pitch as it passes for the Doppler Effect (page 135).

The tongue flutters up and down, across tucked lips.

It may take a little time to develop this rapid up-and-down movement of the tongue (see also the Mouth Mandolin, page 110).

The helicopter sound can be made gradually louder to simulate a landing approach by drawing in greater amounts of air. If made a little breathier, the sound can also be used to imitate birds in flight (see Bird Tweets, Etc., page 62).

SMALL-ARMS FIRE

To make the sound of gunshots, from rifles to shotguns and other small-arms fire, do the following.

INSTRUCTIONS

GUNSHOTS

1. Make a hard, explosive, gravelly "kuh" sound with the back of your tongue and the top rear of your mouth.

2. This a basic gunshot. You can add reverberation and echo, giving it more weight and distance, by shaping your mouth and tongue.

Tongue is arched in back of the mouth.

Make your explosive "kuh," trailing off the sound and shaping your mouth as if you were saying a slow, gliding "eeee-oooo."

3. Rifles and small-arms fire have a sharp crack to them. Pushing the explosive "kuh" forward in your mouth and towards a sharper "kiiii" sound will lighten the armament. Experiment with various trailing sounds to make the right sounding echoes.

Shape mouth as if saying "eeee-ooooo."

SHOTGUNS TO MORTARS ⊙ 66

1. You can make heavier weaponry by adding a simultaneous burst of air from your lips to your "kuuuh" sound. Close your lips and, as you say a forceful "kuh" back in your mouth, say a strong, explosive "b" (or "buh" sound) with your lips.

2. You can mute the sound with your lips for more distant mortars or bring the fire in closer by brightening it. Try letting the explosions trail off as you say a gliding "kee-uuuuu" that slides back into your throat.

THUH-BOOM EXPLOSIONS ⊙66

1. You can create small explosions, as above, or larger ones by first making a spit-sound with your tongue and lips. Try this a few times until you make a quick spit-thud. Thupf. Thupf. Thupf.

2. Thupf-buuuhh! Make a quick spit-thud as the attacking first sound and immediately add to it a large mortar explosion (see Shotguns to Mortars). The more you sustain the sound with a trailing "k" sound in your throat, shaped by an "ohhh-ooooo" in your mouth, the bigger and more distant it will be. Let the echo fall away slowly.

BOMBS ⊙66

Do the famous bomb drop "incoming whistle" with the Invisible Whistle (page 92) or any whistle, really, letting it glide downward in pitch. Into your cupped hands, follow it quickly with a big, slow spit-thud, thuh-booooomm (see Thuh-Booom Explosions, above). Let it trail off, opening your hands slowly.

INCOMING ROCKETS ⊙66

Incoming rockets are a continuous, crackling sound that starts with a crackling little "kee" way back in your throat that quickly builds in volume and drops in pitch as you pull the sound forward in your mouth. Incoming! Incoming!

USES

Putting all the munitions effects together will give you the pitch of battle. Throw in cars, sirens, jets, rockets and planes for added impact.

THE SUBMARINE

1 2 **3** 4 ⦿

66

Submarines, those underwater cigars, produce a wealth of noises that will make excellent additions to your vocal collection.

INSTRUCTIONS

SONAR 1: THE EASY WAY   ⊙66

1. Keep your lips loose and, in a very high, resonant falsetto, make the sound "buuu."

2. Place the palm of one hand against one corner of your mouth. As you produce a series of high-pitched "buuu's," rapidly open and close the hand over your mouth so that the sound has an echoey, tremolo effect.

The hand vibrates rapidly over the mouth to add echo.

SONAR 2: BETTER BUT HARDER   ⊙66

Another way to create sonar is to use the Invisible Whistle (page 92). Make a "p" sound to begin each whistled beat, and end each pip with vibrato.

THE DIVE SIREN   ⊙66

1. Put your lips nearly together. Draw in your lower lip slightly so that your upper teeth rest on your lower lip. (As the siren issues forth, the teeth and lips will muffle it a bit.) In your most nasal falsetto, hum a loud tone. Let it rise and fall rhythmically in pitch and volume as a siren does.

2. Follow the Dive Siren with a guttural "aaa-oooooo—gah," made in a gravelly fashion at the back of your throat.

Teeth on lower lip sharpen tone of falsetto siren.

3. Cup your hands over your mouth to muffle your voice so it sounds like it's coming over a loudspeaker and say in a low-pitched, nasal voice, "Dive, dive, dive . . ." Put the sounds together for some excellent bathtub play.

HUM AND WHISTLE...

Fully titled, the Hum and Whistle Multi-purpose Space Effect is just the thing for zapping your way through steel doors, beaming around ectoplasm, and generally tazing alien life-forms out of existence. It can become the sound of hovering starships and intergalactic communicators. For those of you in need of a death ray, the Hum and Whistle should fill the bill nicely.

INSTRUCTIONS

1. Follow the instructions for the Pucker Whistle (page 90).
2. As you produce the Pucker Whistle, hum a low, steady note.

USES

Once you have perfected the Hum and Whistle, raise and lower the pitch of the whistle while keeping the hum constant. This lends a Hollywood-type eeriness to the sound. Snuggle up close to the ear of a dozing friend and lovingly jolt them with the Hum and Whistle death ray. They may treat you like an alien.

Space Effects

In the futuristic frontiers of space, sounds fly at us as exotic swooshes, fantastic screeches, and dark, resonating ka-booms—at least that's the way Hollywood tells it. And who's to argue? No one can honestly say, "That's not what an Enemy Alien Laser sounds like!"

In reality, closing a door in a space colony may sound exactly like slamming a screen door in Omaha. But that's unimaginative. The wonder of space effects is that they may sound as outrageous and unbelievable as you want.

THE LASER GUN

The Laser Gun forms a fine defense against such cosmic scourges as demon extraterrestrials, enemy star fleets, and dinnertime telemarketers.

INSTRUCTIONS

1. Say the word *cue*. Notice that your tongue touches the roof of your mouth.

2. Repeat the word very slowly, but this time do not finish the word. Keep the tongue on the roof of the mouth and continue to let air rush past. With a sort of rolling motion, slide the tongue back along the roof of your mouth and you will get a rushing "swoosh" of a sound.

Practice until you have what you imagine to be the electronic burst of a laser.

USES

Once you have mastered the Laser Gun, try beginning each "swoosh" by forming your mouth as if you were saying a "th" sound. Start with a "th" and, with a rapid, fluid motion, slide the tongue back to form the "cue" sound. This will give your Laser Gun added punch.

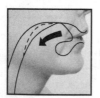

The arched tongue rolls back on the roof of the mouth for the "swoosh" sound.

THE LIGHT SABER

1 2 **3** 4 ◉

67

The *Star Wars* light saber is a classic. Now, for your backyard battle of good versus evil . . .

INSTRUCTIONS

1. Say "oooo," in a low, forceful, resonant voice. Let the volume of the "oo" swell and fade: oooOOOoooo . . . oooOOOoooo . . .
2. Now close your mouth, purse your lips slightly and seal them. Hum again forcefully, but this time your lips should buzz, letting out the escaping air. Still making the deep "ooo" sound, move your tongue forward and backward to change the buzzing, as if you are saying the word *wow*. Experiment and you will be rewarded with a buzzing, swooshing saber.

Hum reinforces vibrating lips.

USES

Try your Light Saber with a flashlight—or maybe brandish a stalk of celery in your cafeteria, and watch people back away from the salad bar.

151

STAR TREK DOORS

Fortunately, the Starship *Enterprise* did not have just ordinary screen doors. The automatic sliding doors on the main bridge are now, and forever will be, awesome. In reality, it was just two guys in the back, yanking apart a couple of painted pieces of plywood, and a cool suction sound effect . . . but magic, it was.

INSTRUCTIONS

1. Put the tip of your tongue lightly through your teeth and suck in air. You will hear a sort of "thhhh" sound.
2. Now, still inhaling air, draw your tongue back

suddenly and say, in a high, ascending voice, something like the word "thoit" on your inhale. Practice and you will hear the mechanical suction sound of Spock going below.

GALACTIC GIZMO

In deep space, machines sound alike. They make a sort of humming, whirring sound that satisfies even the most hardened science-fiction buffs. The Galactic Gizmo is a general-purpose whirr that can be used to imitate an interplanetary assortment of machines, such as spaceships, robots, control boards, and air-lock doors.

INSTRUCTIONS

1. Make the sound of the letter "j."

2. As you make the "j" sound, hum a low-pitched tone to draw out the "j" into a sort of mechanical whirr.

USES

You can perform a pretty good rendition of a robot by slowly and stiffly moving your appendages about to the sound of your gizmo whirr. At the end of each motion, terminate the sound with a sharp "ch" or "chk" sound. Use your robot for a nice entrance into English class or a budget-control meeting, or simply to disrupt gatherings and coolly harass others.

THE WATER DRIP

Household Sounds

The household is a treasure trove of little sounds:
The blender whirrs, the back door slams,
the bacon sizzles, the printer jams,
the toilet gurgles, the drawer klunks,
the fan is buzzing, toss-the-trash . . . ker-plunk.

Drip. Drop. Drip. That persistent little plop of a water drop. Drip. Drop. Drip. There is something so delicate—a touch of percussion, a hint of liquid round-ness. Such drips measure time—they carve mountains into canyons and they keep us awake at night. But more than anything, they are music, pure and simple. The Water Drip is a classic mouth sound effect.

INSTRUCTIONS

1. Close off the back of your mouth by breathing normally through your nose. Draw your tongue to the back of your mouth, as if you were holding water in your mouth. Shape your lips into a whistle-pucker, with about an ⅛-inch round hole in the center of your lips.

2. Now push your tongue forward quickly and raise the floor of your mouth (as if you're pushing water out of your mouth) so that you force a little burst of air through your puckered lips to produce a slight whistle.

Practice this until you get the slightest hint of little whistle tone produced solely by the action of your tongue pushing air forward. (Do *not* whistle by blowing out air from your lungs, as in a normal whistle.)

3. Breathing through your nose, now thump lightly on the hollow of your cheek to create a single "Ploit" (see the Ploit Principle, page 24). Your tongue should be well back and your lips in a whistle-pucker. Just as you thump on your cheek, push the tongue forward to make the whistle. *Drip!*

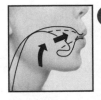

The tongue pushes forward with the lips puckered to produce a whistle . . .

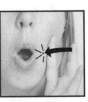

. . . and a well-timed thump on the cheek makes the drip.

USES

The Water Drip can be quite realistic. To impress or confuse, you can use it completely out of context: in the classroom, in the dentist's waiting room, at dinner, or over cocktails. Or, use it in context, for personal amusement, in a bathroom stall. The Water Drip becomes quite impressive when amplified by a microphone or telephone.

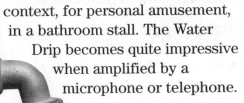

155

AQUARIUM EFFECT

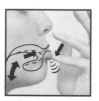

People love the sound of a bubbling aquarium, but hate dealing with the scum, algae, stinky rainbow gravel, and tropical fish that bloat and float. Here, you can keep the bubbles and lose the overhead with your own Aquarium Effect.

INSTRUCTIONS

1. Close off the back of your mouth by breathing normally through your nose. Poke out your bottom lip as if you are pouting.

2. Take the finger of one hand and let it flip down on the lower lip to make the lip snap back against the upper lip with a little popping sound. Widen the back of your mouth and move your tongue forward and backward to maximize the pop and change its tone.

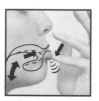

Back of mouth closed; finger snaps lips.

3. Once you feel comfortable with your single lip-pop, use the four fingertips of one hand to brush down across your bottom lip. Rotate your fingers down across your lip, starting with the tip of the little finger and rolling fluidly to the tip of the index finger. You should get a sequence of four quick bubble-like sounds.

Moving your fingers in sequence produces a bubbling sound.

4. Do the same sequence of pops, strumming your lips with your other hand. By quickly alternating hands, you can get a continuous sequence of bubbly pops.

USES

Add depth to your effervescent bubbles by shifting your tongue back and forth in your mouth, simultaneously lowering and raising the floor of your mouth. (Do not move your jaw, only the muscles on the floor of your mouth and throat.) The pitch of the bubbles will rise and fall. Use this sound in fishing stories and for the Sink (page 157).

THE SINK

The sound of a sink draining in a summer house is a carefree, musical one, especially since you don't have to worry about the plumbing—it's a rental.

INSTRUCTIONS

1. Whisper the word *cue* in slow motion, and notice how your tongue and lips glide slowly forward. (Diction coaches would call that a "gliding diphthong," but we won't—it just sounds too nasty.)

2. Now do the same thing, but inhale as you say it. Let the word slide from the front of your mouth to the very back and down into your throat. That's the first part of the sink drain.

3. For the gurgle at the end, finish this draining sound off with an Inhaled Glottal Fry (page 27) in a gentle, continuous sound.

4. For the coup de grâce, seal the sound with a few bubbles from the Aquarium Effect (page 156).

THE BLOW-DRYER

1 2 **3** 4 ●

68

Every morning, lights dim all over the country as millions of damp-haired Americans subject themselves to the searing, whirring, and whining of a pistol-grip, 1,800-watt blow-dryer. Here's how you can do the "Blow-Dryer: Unplugged."

INSTRUCTIONS

1. To make the sound of a hair dryer, you must first master the Fingerless Whistle (page 96). This is the only hard part. Follow the directions for the whistle, but blow gently, making a fairly low-pitched, soft whistle.

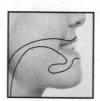

The tongue is arched off the floor of the mouth.

2. As you whistle, hum a long, low note. The combination of the whistle and hum makes a very realistic blow-dryer imitation. Glide upward in pitch as you start. You can even change speeds on your blow-dryer from "blow" to "destroy" by suddenly increasing the pitch of your hum and whistle, blowing you off a chair.

USES

Use the Blow-Dryer to bamboozle others. Walk up behind an attractive someone and, as a conversation starter, begin blow-drying his or her locks. You're guaranteed a reaction. Or, instead of merely combing your hair in a store window reflection, add blow-drying to your grooming ritual. If you happen to be bored in a drugstore, walk over to the hair-dryer display, pick up a sample, and proceed to style your hair with the unplugged dryer. It is so realistic, the sales clerk will be speechless.

The Blow-Dryer effect can also be used to imitate a wide range of other whirring gadgets from vacuum cleaners to blenders, and even spinning tires in the snow (see Spinning Tires, page 136).

FIRE EXTINGUISHER

Ready. Aim. Fire extinguisher! This is a sound that, for everyday use, is undeniably more fun than the real thing. (More fun, that is, until there's a real fire.)

INSTRUCTIONS

1. Open your mouth and throat wide. Forcefully exhale air and make a strong gagging sound, deep in your throat. This is the CO_2 rushing out.
2. Now squeeze it off by pushing the rear floor of your mouth upward, as if you're hawking a loogy (or, more explicitly, spitting out phlegm). There's your squeeze-off.

USES

Mime extinguishing candles this way. Or, in place of an opening line, approach the backside of some hottie and mime-extinguish the heat. *Or,* try performing songs like "Frère Jacques" or "Twinkle, Twinkle Little Star" while holding a real extinguisher—until fire marshals shut down the joint.

TOUCH DIALING

The touch-tone phone was first introduced in 1963, and has since become the standard. Does anyone even remember the pre-digital days before voicemail and touch-tone thickets . . . "if your emergency is of a personal nature, press . . ."? Though this sound is a bit of a challenge at first, once you master it, your vocal touch-tone will be . . . untouchable.

INSTRUCTIONS

1. First, do an Invisible Whistle (page 92). Make little short whistles, turning them into little tones of varying pitches. Begin each tone with your mouth closed. Keep your lips very loose.

2. Whistle in bursts, letting the air puff out the lips and blow them open. This gives the sound some interesting added tones and a sharp attack. You can make tones with a high falsetto voice, but it's very difficult for most people.

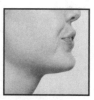

Let whistle puff out from loose lips.

USES

The Tele-Mime: For all phone effects, a good Tele-Mime phone is useful. Make a loose fist, then open out your thumb and your pinky finger only. Place the thumb near your ear and the extended pinky finger near your mouth to create a makeshift phone receiver. With your other hand, dial the imaginary phone.

ROTARY DIALING

R otary dialing has gone by the wayside, except in old movies and tag sales. But it remains a classic mechanical sound. (We forget where the "dial" in "phone dialing" comes from.) Here it is, for preservation purposes.

INSTRUCTIONS

1. With lips slightly open, clench your teeth and draw the tongue to the back of the mouth.

2. Now blow out sharply through your teeth to make a hissing sound. As you make this hiss, forcefully ram the tongue forward to seal it against the back of the teeth, abruptly halting the hiss.

Blow through clenched teeth for a hiss and thrust your tongue forward . . .

3. With the tongue fully forward, quickly follow the hiss with a series of clicking sounds. Create these little sucking sounds between the tongue and the front roof of your mouth. Each rushing hiss is followed by varying numbers of clicking sounds.

. . . followed by a quick series of clicks made with sucking motions of your tongue.

CELL PHONE RING

Cell phone rings come at us in all forms and from all directions. On the silent setting, they even vibrate in our pants. Now you can add your very own version to the mix.

INSTRUCTIONS

1. Roll an "r" on the roof of your mouth, like the rolling of a Spanish or Scottish "rrrrr."
2. Now bring your top lip down tightly over your upper front teeth so that its taut, inside edge lies just inside your upper teeth.

Tongue vibrates against tucked upper lip.

3. Roll the "r" again on the roof of your mouth, then push it forward to roll on your top lip (still tucked over your top teeth). You should hear a gentle rolling sound.
4. As you do this rolling tongue on your inside upper lip, hum in a high, falsetto voice. You should hear a little electronic-sounding beeping chirp. Work with the sound until it sounds like an incoming cell phone call.

USES

You can use this fake cell call to get you off unpleasant landline phone calls—"B-b-b-b-b-beep!! Gotta go, my other phone is ringing . . ." Or do the Cell Phone Ring, then pull out and fake-answer your real cell phone—to get out of any sticky situation. Someone can appear to reach out and touch you, just when you need it.

THE PHONE VOICE

The effect of the Phone Voice on the other end can be very convincing, particularly if you don't move your lips very much as you perform it.

INSTRUCTIONS

1. To simulate a voice on the other end of any phone call, use the Vent Voice (see page 208). This voice is muted by your arched tongue and does not appear to be coming from your mouth.
2. For the sound of ringing coming over the phone, simply roll a Spanish "r" gently on the roof of your mouth, with a little click at the end for the pick-up.

THE CANNED EFFECT

A very convincing way to call someone over the phone and appear to be a pre-recorded message is by talking slightly into and across a large drinking glass or big plastic cup (see Robot Voice, page 215). Over-articulate your words and speak in your best announcer voice. You can also use this technique to simulate the voice on the other end of a phone for radio plays and recordings.

USES

Use the Tele-Mime hand mentioned earlier (see Rotary Dialing, page 161), the vocal phone dial, the ring and pick-up, and this Voice on the other end, and you can have a complete telephone conversation with someone, on a totally invisible phone. Or . . . "Excuse me. Do you have painful, burning sensations? . . ."

Use the Canned Effect to telemarket fake products and dream vacations to friends, hawk political candidates, and so on. If you really want to push the limits, try calling friends with courtesy "wake-up calls."
Warning: Don't try tele-pranks on strangers—they are now armed with caller ID, and you could end up getting wake-up calls yourself . . . from the authorities.

THE HAND SAW

The sound of the suburban hand saw is a kind of Home Depot mating call or, more likely, a cry for professional help.

INSTRUCTIONS

1. Make a "guh" sound on the roof of your mouth (see the Palate Grind, page 25). Now inhale and exhale this Palate Grind, making it as gravelly as possible.

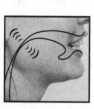

Along with a falsetto whine, produce Palate Grinds in back of the mouth.

2. To make the rasp of the saw, separately make a high falsetto tone that glides up in pitch. Now inhale and exhale your Palate Grind and combine it with the exhale this high rasp for each downstroke of the saw.

USES

Of course, no saw sound is complete without a back-and-forth sawing motion of your arms. Using an ordinary knife and fork, use the saw imitation at a meal to hint that, perhaps, the steak is tough. Or inflict psychological damage on your spouse, kid brother, or classmate by "sawing" through various sections of her midriff or limbs. At your next party, you might try "sawing" a lady in half.

DOOR KNOCKS

You can add Door Knocks (also useful for the sound of hammer hits) to your effects and stories. It's easy. Really.

INSTRUCTIONS

1. Simply force out a strong "bfff . . . bff . . . bfff . . ." to blow the lips open.

2. Combine it with a strong Palate Grind (page 25) on the roof of your mouth. With practice you can nail it.

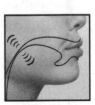

Force air out to blow lips open.

PIZZA

Fresh Taste at a Great Price!

WE USE ONLY THE FINEST INGREDIENTS.

THE TENNIS MATCH

The sound of two titans, battling swats across the net is actually a rhythmic variant of the Smock (page 186)—just add your own top spin and high lob.

INSTRUCTIONS

1. Breathing through your nose to close off the back of your mouth, seal your lips together.

2. Now abruptly pull them apart by opening your mouth while sucking in air. The effect is a single motion, much like a gigantic "smack."

3. Rhythm is important to the game. Do a single, loud "smok" (a serve), then a bounce-hit of the return— smok, smak—two sounds, tight together. Then a beat (as the ball flies over the net), then another return— smok, smak—and so forth, until a call of "out!" from the line judge. Follow the ball with your head and give your best tennis strokes with an imaginary racket. Forty–love.

Seal lips tightly while breathing through nose.

Pull lips apart while sucking in air.

THE BOWLING ALLEY

The Bowling Alley is an amazing sound effect at close range or when delivered over the phone or close to the ear of a loved one. It's the sound of a ball bowled down a hardwood lane, followed by the strike and rattle of the pins—all as a kind of ambient, background sound.

INSTRUCTIONS

1. Whisper a long, extended "kuh-ooooo" sound, the "kuh" part being the sharp drop of the ball, and the "ooooo" being the roll down the hardwood alley. Move your tongue around a bit to vary the rolling sound.

2. For the strike and scatter of the pins, make a stronger, higher pitched "kaahhh" sound, still in a sort of whisper that echoes and fades.

Arena Cheers and Applause

(No difficulty rating. It cannot be taught.) ◉ 71

One of the sound effect classics, passed on from father to son, is the sound of stadium crowds going crazy. It's the personal sound effect you use when you shoot hoops alone. It's for when your team's down by two, with three seconds on the clock and you sink one from downtown. Swish! Thirteen thousand adoring fans in your head rise to their feet, wild with excitement. A kind of breathy, white-noise whisper issues forth from your throat—eeeeaaaaaahhhhhh!—and you begin jumping, instinctively, in slow motion, down the length of your driveway. Waves of applause follow, as a kind of hissing sound flows past your lips. These are not sound effects that can be taught in the mere pages of a book like this. They must be learned at the feet of a wise and patient master.

167

RUDE NOISES

BEYOND INNER RUDENESS

Rudeness, as an existential concept, is a satisfying indifference to what is generally accepted to be good form. It can range from the inelegant to the offensive, from the discourteous to the indecent. Rudeness can be tasteless, uncivilized, insolent, or just plain malodorous.

But rudeness is not an act. It is a state of mind, an attitude. Rudeness exists in its own right—in the intent of the initiator. The implication here is that even if we are absolutely alone, we can still officially be disgusting. This is a comforting thought. We can find our own Inner Rudeness. Ripping one alone at midnight can be just as satisfyingly rude as slipping one at Tiffany's.

Quite often, however, we would like to tell a certain someone to go suck an egg or eat our shorts, but our upbringing, the pressures of society, and general decorum restrain us. Because our vocabulary is limited, we may be forced to deny ourselves the added pleasure of displaying our Inner Rudeness to others.

The purpose, then, of this chapter is to help you expand your vocabulary from traditional words and actions into the ever-so-subtle realm of crude and offensive noises. By incorporating these noises into your own rubric of rudeness, you can better exercise and satisfy the more barbaric undercurrents of your psyche—and, thereby, move beyond your own (cue the fading echo) INNER RUDENESS . . . NESS . . . Ness . . . ness . . . ness.

THE RASPBERRY

Let's get down to basics. Body sounds are a part of life. Although we may try to cover them up, push them down, or deny them, they are with us every step of the way.

Body sounds are an inescapable part of the life process. Our best strategy is not to treat them as ugly stepchildren, but to embrace them whole-heartedly and bring them into our service.

The Raspberry or Bronx Cheer (or dare we say fart*) is the granddaddy of body sounds. From the time Roman senators first used it to pooh-pooh fellow senators, the Raspberry has been a part of our society. Chaucer, Shakespeare, and Faulkner are just a few of the literary giants whose characters wheel and deal in raspberries.

Psychologically, the Raspberry is the poor man's protest. Even a person in the most powerless position can, at minimum, give authority a good "razz."

The Raspberry is legal. It makes a point and, if nothing else, is personally therapeutic.

INSTRUCTIONS

1. Close your mouth, stick your tongue through your lips, and then force out air. "Phlbbb." What a fine sound, full of history and tradition.
2. Complement the basic Raspberry by placing the thumb of your opened hand against your nose and waggling the fingers to add a little more insult (see opposite page).

USES

The Raspberry (with the hand flourish) is perfect behind the backs of authority figures—parents, teachers, business superiors, flight attendants, parole officers, and Congressmen. If performed while their backs are turned, authorities are none the wiser, and you score points with your colleagues for launching the modest protest. Be creative. Use the Raspberry to signal a slow waiter for the check, wave good-bye to a mother-in-law, or provocatively signal a good-looker in a singles bar.

---

*Fart Euphemisms:

Break wind, bottom burp, pass wind, let rip, cut the cheese, blow the butt bugle, trouser cough, airbrush your boxers, under burp, lay an air biscuit, lay a stinky, fire a stink torpedo, party in your pants, poot, step on a frog, toot, strangle the stank monkey, heinous anus, doing the one-cheek sneak, back belch, sbd, barking spider, pass gas, the f-bomb, rectal roar, anal salute, invert-a-burp, trouser tuba, fire the retro-rocket, release a squeaker.

EROTIC RASPBERRY

The Erotic Raspberry is the most social of all raspberries, since it takes a team of two to pull it off—a razzer and a razzee. It is usually a sign of affection between consenting adults. You might be surprised at how much a crowd loves an Erotic Raspberry delivered between the shoulder blades of a beautiful woman in a strapless evening gown. (Although it may take a few days for the swelling on your face to go down.)

INSTRUCTIONS

1. After a proper introduction, the razzer gently requests exposure of a body part, usually the stomach and occasionally the back, of the razzee.

2. When given the nod, the razzer lifts up the shirt or blouse of the razzee, places his or her mouth on the soft part, and then blows out forcefully. *Razzzz!*

USES

The Erotic Raspberry takes on a liquidy quality if produced in the shower, and a greasy, sliding quality if attempted at surf-side with the aid of suntan lotion. Though sneak attacks with family and friends are fun, public attempts of the Erotic Raspberry are discouraged—and certainly illegal in red states.

THE WOOZIE

The Woozie, or "zerbert" in some circles, is a harmless variation of the Erotic Raspberry. It is executed exclusively on the stomachs of fat babies by their parents and child-care professionals and is officially sanctioned by most local authorities. The Woozie is one of the main reasons adults continue to have offspring (what with the upkeep and all).

THE TRANSPARENT WOOZIE

The Transparent Woozie is, as its name suggests, a variation on the Woozie. It is nearly silent, but dreadfuly shocking because of its surpise execution.

The Transparent Woozie requires three items: a transparent piece of glass (such as a window or a windshield), a viewer or viewers on the other side of the glass (preferably of the unsuspecting variety), and a set of lips (which you should have with you at all times).

INSTRUCTIONS

1. When presented with the appropriate configuration of items—let's say a friend inside a parked Toyota or on the other side of the window of a Kentucky Fried Chicken—you, as the Woozie-person, press your open mouth directly on the glass and blow like heck. If executed correctly, your cheeks should puff out like balloons, and the viewer inside will suddenly see the inside of your entire mouth,

splayed out across the glass. It's ugly. The beauty is the surprise.

2. As the Woozie-person, you then detach yourself from the glass, wipe it clean with your sleeve, and walk on.

3. Wait for your cell phone to ring.

Cockney Rhyming and Raspberries

How did we come to use the word *raspberry* as a euphemism for flatulence? It's derived from cockney rhyming slang, that colorful language from East London, where "goin' up the apples" means "goin' up the *stairs*" (apples and *pears*), "picking up me teapots" means "picking up my *kids*" (teapot lids), and "goin' home to me troubles" means "going home to my *wife*" (troubles and *strife*). Raspberries? Raspberry *tart.*

173

THE FIZZLE RAZZ

The Fizzle Razz does not have the rich tradition of the Raspberry, but it is certainly nastier and more offensive.

INSTRUCTIONS

1. Pull your lower lip into your mouth and place your upper teeth firmly over it.

2. Force air out through one corner of your mouth to produce a particularly deep and ugly razz with your upper lip.

Experiment with varying lip tensions and air pressure to develop your own distinct, rude, spluttering sound.

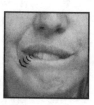

With your teeth over your lower lip, blow out the side of your mouth.

USES

The Fizzle Razz is a direct affront, delivered as a face-to-face assault. It does not involve words, and can be used in heated arguments in place of verbal insults that could be used against you in court. (Sadly, the Fizzle Razz is much underused in debates by political candidates.)

But do be discreet in wielding the Fizzle Razz. It is pedal-to-the-metal powerful. You can wind up having your lips ripped off.

STOMACH GROWLS

Stomach growls are cosmic. They are those little whirr-and-whistle messages from the inner sanctum of our digestive tracts. They are cryptic communications from the galaxy within us. Stomach growls are uncontrollable, unpredictable, and, in a quiet room, undeniable. They are almost always funny. And oddly enough, unlike other plumbing problems, they are actually accepted and chuckled at in polite company.

INSTRUCTIONS

Say the word *oreo*.* Now *inhale* and say the word *oreo*. (If you have trouble, see the Inhaled Fry (page 27). Inhale "oreo-oooo" and let the pitch glide downward as you pull it far back into your throat. Keep your mouth almost closed.

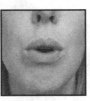

Mouth nearly closed; throat opened wide.

USES

Just like real stomach growls, your simulations should be low and subtle and reserved for intimate, quiet moments. If you suddenly get to an awkward topic of conversation, use the Stomach Growl to create a temporary diversion. Act good-naturedly surprised, apologize profusely, and quickly change the subject. The effect can be a lifesaver during sticky business lunches and delicate social situations.

*Author's Note:

I wish that the word *oreo* was, in fact, product placement, for which I'd be rolling in dough. Unfortunately, it has nothing to do with the Nabisco cookie—it just happens to be the word that works. (If the folks at Nabisco were up for it, however, I'd be more than happy to change the word to *Wheat Thins*.)

THE ERSATZ BURP

Burps, those guttural fireworks, are always lurking somewhere in the depths of us. The fuse is lit with 16-ounce soft drinks, sausage pizza, Rice-A-Roni, shrimp creole, baby back ribs, or fast-food tacos. Then suddenly, when we least expect it—*burrrrrrp!* We may try to swallow it, stifle it, or run for cover. It's no use: Despite all efforts, the burp explodes in all its auditory wonder.

In some cultures a resounding burp is a sign of gastronomic enjoyment; in others, it will get you taken off the invitation list. But we should be proud of the burp. It is an audible affirmation that we are alive and processing. In all cases, it is our wild side trying to get out, which is why the burp is the archenemy of teachers, orchestra conductors, and society matrons—anyone who imposes order on others.

The Ersatz Burp is a refined simulation of the real burp. It is quite unlike the emanations of grammar school cutups who gulp down bushels of air and then belch loudly upon command. That is, to be sure, a finely honed skill, but it doesn't have the controlled elegance of the Ersatz Burp.

INSTRUCTIONS

1. Practice the Inhaled Fry (page 27). Open your throat as wide as possible and produce as deep an Inhaled Fry as you can.

2. Try bursting out in a low "errr" sound. Then try articulating the sound "breep."

With a little work, you can develop a resonant artificial burp that would shock your mother.

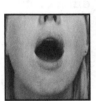

Your mouth open wide adds resonance and quality.

Mouth shaped to say "errr."

USES

Picture yourself on a plane or bus, sitting next to a talkative woman with body odor. The situation is clearly unbearable, but you have the window seat and don't want to move. Solution? The Ersatz Burp.

As the woman jabbers on about her childhood in Milwaukee and the latest illness of a pet, burp. That will stop conversation momentarily. Fake an apology, then burp again. Act disturbed, and mention something about motion sickness. Lean toward her. Cover your mouth and get very quiet. Whammo. The woman will quietly excuse herself, and you can then sleep, gaze out the window, or read in privacy.

The Ersatz Burp is just the ticket whenever a whiff of anarchy is needed. It is a male bonding thing, a must for an overly intense chemistry class, and perfect for loosening up a stuffy staff meeting.

THE NOSE BLOW

One of those little rituals of the winter season is blowing your nose. In the past, we waited for a private moment, extracted a neatly folded handkerchief, unfolded it methodically, placed it over the nose, and blew discreetly into its monogrammed folds. But times have changed.

Now whenever we get the urge, we yank out a crumpled Kleenex, slap it to our face, and let it rip. Genteel nasal clearing may be a thing of the past. But so much the better. This gives you added creative possibilities in using your artificial Nose Blow.

INSTRUCTIONS

1. Keeping the front of your tongue on the floor or your mouth, arch the middle of your tongue upward to touch the roof of your slightly opened mouth.

2. Blow out air so that it flows *under* the tongue. You should get a gravelly, "razzing" sound as the bottom of the tongue vibrates against the floor of your mouth. Experiment with this, and listen to the CD.

Blow air under your tongue for a nose-blowing sound.

3. Cup your hands over your mouth and nose, and produce your under-the-tongue "razz." It should sound like, as your doctor might say, a "productive" Nose Blow.

USES

You can use the Nose Blow for a gag, equaled in effect only by plastic vomit and spring-loaded chewing-gum tricks. Spying your victim, compliment him on his tie and lift it up admiringly for a closer look. Press it to your face and simulate your robust Nose Blow. What a fine way to set the tone for an office Christmas party.

Another use of the Nose Blow sounds horrible in print, but done right, will give unsuspecting spectators vapor lock. Next time you're among good friends, casually remove a clean handkerchief, unfold it, artificially Nose Blow into it, and then without ever removing it from your face, appear to mop your face with it. "Did he just do what I think he did?" flashes across everyone's minds. It's guaranteed to get a rise.

THE SPLAT

In the vast sea of sound around us, some distinctive noises bob to the surface—those that are unsavory, disgusting, or otherwise repulsive. They have the ability to conjure up images of viscous, gooey things, puffy body parts, and nasty situations involving ooze. Because generally disgusting sounds have such emotional presence, they make excellent additions to your vocal menagerie.

The Splat, for instance, is used by nature to indicate the moment of impact of any gelatinous blob. It is the sound of custard pie in the face, meat loaf dropped to the floor from waist level, or wet flounder thrown against the wall.

Clearly, the Splat qualifies for inclusion in the Disgusting Sound Hall of Fame.

INSTRUCTIONS

1. Draw your tongue back into your mouth as far as possible.

2. Tense your lips into a slight pucker. Blow air through them in such a way that they vibrate to produce a moderate "buzz."

3. As you make the "buzz," ram your tongue forward to reduce the cavity within your mouth. Push your tongue quickly all the way

The tongue is pushed forward through buzzing lips.

forward and out between your buzzing lips to create the Splat effect. Splats can be long and disgustingly drawn out or short and quick. Try variations.

4. To add more gelatinous weight to your splat, draw out the buzzing of your lips by pushing your tongue forward more slowly. At the same time, add a strong, low hum at the same pitch as your lip buzz. Your splat will become a slow oozing sound with an even higher gross-out factor.

USES

The Splat is a fine, general-purpose effect that should be slipped into conversation during appropriate (or, for that matter, inappropriate) moments. You can also do a shortened version —the goose "phut-phut"—to imitate the sound of a flock of Canada geese grazing on a golf course or highway median. (See Goose Honk, page 42.)

Informed Sound-Making and Throw-Up ⊙77

There is a world of difference between amateurs and alert, trained soundmakers when it comes to creating a convincing up-chuck or throw-up sound. From time to time, a trouble-making ten-year-old will attempt to clear a darkened movie theater or a school cafeteria with a fake vomit sound—a feeble gagging sound that fools no one, and serves only to get him swiftly and quietly removed by the 24-plex management or the on-duty PE teacher.

The informed soundmaker, however—perhaps a reader of this book—will notice and perform two specific details that will make his version of the sound spring to life. First, he will take a swig of a carbonated beverage, swishing it rapidly in his mouth to "make it foam up big time." Second, he will swallow a bit of air, and as he fakes a gagging sound, he will encourage the air to rise up and out as burp, creating the impression of stomach momentum. He will gag, cough, and let the small amount of carbonated foam flop out of his mouth and spatter to the floor. (If you are thinking that this is unsanitary, you should be reminded that the floor is already sticky with Gummy Worms and spent Twizzlers.) General restlessness will ensue, alarm will grow, and some screaming is possible as patrons head for the doors. After a while, the trained soundmaker is presented the ultimate prize—a guy shows up with rubber gloves and a bucket of pine-scented cleaner.

LABORED BREATHING

Remember: If you are thinking filthy thoughts now, you are probably breaking the law in a Republican state somewhere. Labored Breathing, that mark of obscene phone callers around the world, does not have to be obscene at all. It can be put to good use.

INSTRUCTIONS

1. Rest your tongue on the bottom lip of your opened mouth.
2. Make a very low, groaning "aah" sound and breathe heavily, both in and out. Congratulations. This is Labored Breathing. (If you have asthma, and do this already, I'm sorry your time was wasted.)

USES

Labored Breathing can be used for brilliant effect in one particular case: as telemarketer repellent. The next time you get a telephone solicitation, lay some heavy, labored breathing on the guy as he speaks. He'll be thoroughly creeped out and won't call again.

Elevator Gag

Labored Breathing is also quite effective in elevators. . . . Elevators are an anomaly in our world. For a few seconds, we are locked into a tiny room with total strangers. What better time to take advantage of your fellow man than that unique moment of vulnerability?

With an accomplice, walk into a crowded elevator. Stoop a bit and produce your best Labored Breathing. Your friend should stand beside you with his or her mouth and nose covered with a handkerchief. Through the muffle of the protective cloth, the accomplice asks in a voice loud enough for all to hear: "Just what exactly did the doctor say you had?"

As you continue to breathe loudly, all other breathing on the elevator will stop. When the doors next open, there is usually a mass exodus or, at the very least, a group of elevator riders with bulging eyes and a bluish tinge to their faces.

GUMMY CHEEKS

Gummy Cheeks is a juicy, abstract sound that slips past "mildly unpleasant" on the gross-factor rating scale and slides straight for "downright filthy"—in the way that stirring tuna and mayo together in a bowl has a disgusting sound, but you're not quite sure why. Gummy Cheeks does not simulate any one sound in particular, but rather suggests a whole host of offensive goings-on.

INSTRUCTIONS

1. Relax your face completely with your mouth closed loosely.
2. Pinch your cheek lightly with the thumb and crook of the index finger.

3. Pull out and push in the relaxed cheek very rapidly. You will get a repulsive, gooey, slurpy sound—a misdemeanor in Florida.

USES

If you are fortunate enough to have large jowls, your Gummy Cheeks can make grown men squeamish. You can double the indignity by making Gummy Cheeks simultaneously on both cheeks for a sort of slushy, surround-sound effect.

Cheek pinched and moved rapidly back and forth.

THE BOING

The Boing is a sound popularized by Saturday-morning cartoons. It is the reverberating wallop of a frying pan on the head, a coyote leaping with bed-spring shoes, and the sudden rake-in-the-face from a wise-cracking rooster's careless step. The Boing is not a natural sound we encounter in our daily lives. It is the product of the cartoon animator's fertile imagination.

INSTRUCTIONS

1. The Boing is produced by pronouncing the word *boing* in a deep, exaggerated fashion. To make the vibrating quality of the "boing," say "boy-oi-oi-ng" in a drawn-out manner. Create the "oi's" by rapidly pushing the tongue slightly forward and backward in your mouth. It may take practice to develop the proper speed of your "oi's."

The tongue moves back and forth rapidly.

2. Cup your hands over your mouth and nose as you say your "boy-oi-oi-ng," and rapidly open and close the cup, by shaking one hand from the hinges of your wrist. This hand action gives added echo to your Boing.

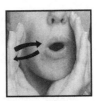

Open and close cupped hands to add an echo.

USES

Use the Boing to spruce up your conversational chatter. When you have a bright idea, preface it with a Boing. Try answering the phone with a Boing instead of the traditional "hello." For those callers who do not hang up, the Boing will be well appreciated as a frank revelation of your mental state.

For a fun alternative to the mouth Boing, see the Jaw Harp (page 129).

185

THE SMOCK

The Smock is a sound rooted squarely in the abstract expressionist school of mouth sounds. It represents no particular sound from life, but is rather a fanciful flight into the world of vaguely suggestive sounds.

INSTRUCTIONS

1. Breathing through your nose to close off the back of your mouth, seal your lips together.
2. Abruptly pull them apart by opening your mouth while sucking in air. The effect is a single motion, much like a gigantic "smack."

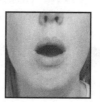

Sealed together, the lips are sucked into the mouth . . .

. . . and the mouth is then abruptly opened.

USES

The Smock resembles the sound of a toilet plunger on a baby's stomach, or, oddly enough, someone walking in wooden clogs. It forms the base for the Tennis Match (page 166). It may also be used to simulate the removal of a suction dart from your brother's (or sister's) forehead. You can use the Smock in rapid repetition as a general-purpose noise to irritate family, teachers, or coworkers.

THE MUD TRUDGE

Kids adore it. Mothers abhor it. Six-year-olds play patty-cake in it. The ultra-chic use it for facials. But whether or not we yearn for that magic moment of childhood when it first oozed up, warm between our toes, mud is tracked through the life of each and every one of us.

Most of the time mud lies quietly, but when we get a chance to walk through it, it sucks at our heels with its slurpy, guttural voice. The Mud Trudge is a gloopy, thick, rich, raw sound that suggests many possibilities, none of which is clean.

INSTRUCTIONS

1. Breathing through your nose, place your flattened tongue on the roof of your mouth loosely.
2. As you slowly open your mouth, draw in air so that your inner cheeks vibrate against the side edge of your tongue. Fully open your mouth so that as you pull your tongue from the roof of your mouth, a wet suction sound oozes between the back of your tongue and cheeks. Practice this (in privacy), working toward a smooth, easy motion—with good suction—that produces the gooey sound of mud.

The back of the tongue is drawn from the roof of the mouth as air passes around its sides.

USES

Your Mud Trudge can be used to simulate the sound of dog food glopping out of a can or the sound of a toilet plunger in action. With the Mud Trudge you can add a colorful sound effect to the serving of mashed potatoes at your next family gathering. Or pull away from that kiss on your aunt's cheek with a resounding Mud Trudge. She'll thank ya for it.

CHAPTER 9

CREATING VOICES

"A duck walks into a bar . . ." Let's say you want that duck to talk. This would be your chapter.

You can learn to stretch your own voice to create new voices, as a natural extension of the MouthSounds taught earlier. Using pitch, placement, position, push, and other vocal effects, get ready to uncover entirely new, surprisingly useful voices—voices for all kinds of performances, from very private to very public, from telephone to television.

YOUR VOCAL SUITCASE

Character voices are vocal costumes you can carry with you anywhere and slip into at just the right moments: for campfire storytelling, bedtime stories, public speeches, classrooms, family meals, jokes, and little moments of private conversation. They are absolutely required for serious acting, animation, and puppeteering—for comedy and drama, on television, in commercials, on air, on stage, and in film.

Teachers and preachers, actors and comedians, professional speakers, performers, storytellers, and politicians—all have varying, trained abilities to create voices. But we all do this to some extent already. Without thinking, we load and fire off different voices, like artillery, to energize our exchanges, beef up our vocabulary and tell stories with impact. (See the box titled "Women, Men, and Voices," on page 195.) The voices we carry with us range from subtle shadings of our normal speaking voice—for emphasizing our pleasure, disgust, warmth, anger, or humor—to dead-on impressions of friends, teachers, bosses, politicians, and anyone else we care to poke fun at.

But Why, Daddy?

You might want to create a special voice for a creative project—a presentation, a story, a performance, a play. Or you might simply want to acquire a range of voices to fill your vocal coat pocket so that you can brandish them at will like good sleight-of-hand. Being able to slip into another voice gives you the ability to ambush your audience and say things in a manner that's far from predictable. You will surprise. You will delight and entertain. You will spin an ordinary sentence into something quite spectacular.

More Lip

Wrapping your voice around new character voices takes every bit of skill you can muster. The mouth sounds you've learned

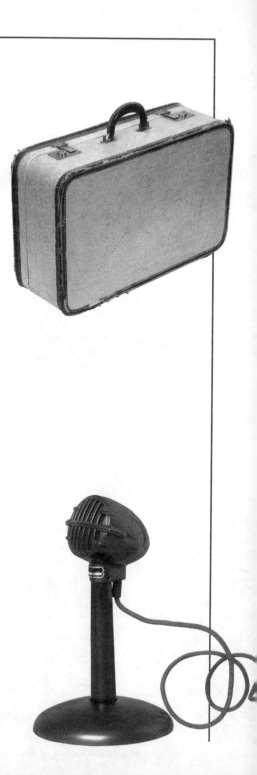

already are like sonic punctuations—they are vocal aerobics that get you to listen better, loosen up, and maybe get you honking a little, too. But creating your own *character voices* involves a more complex grammar, one that uses bits of everything you have ever heard. You may fish from the wide ocean of pop culture that washes over us, or, more reflectively, draw from your personal well of memory, basing voices on the enduring characters of your own life. Either way, with just a little practice, entirely new voices can leap, newborn, from you.

STALKING THE WILD VOICE: HUNTING VS. GATHERING

First of all, if you don't already, begin to notice the richness of human voices around you, more distinctive and varied than any sounds on earth. Since we are born imitators, you will start to absorb the accents and voices you hear. As in sound-making, creating voices requires you to develop an awareness of the voices around you, and of your own voice as you shape its possibilities.

Voice Hunting

Voice hunting is hearing a voice, and then shooting at that vocal target. Whether you actually hit that voice is immaterial (except, perhaps, in the case of impersonations and impressions; see sidebar on page 194). It is the process of shooting *at* a voice— pushing your voice in the direction of a definite voice—that creates new possibilities.

You may begin by hearing a character or voice inside your head, or you may hear something intriguing in the voice of a friend, a stranger, or a cartoon character that suggests a character voice to you. Essentially, in voice hunting, you begin with some quality or notion of what your voice should sound like. (Many character actors report hearing a voice on the street and then following that voice—that person—for blocks, just to hear it and "get it in their head." That's true voice stalking.) Then you try imitating out loud the voice you have in mind. You experiment with your voice and push it in new ways to hear all the possibilities open to you. You must be fearless.

Hunting for Bear

Actor Marlon Brando was said to have based many of his most famous characters on animals and animal behavior. His famous *Godfather* role, for instance, may have drawn on the qualities of a bear.

Voice Gathering

The second approach, voice gathering, is more playful. It is simply stumbling about to see what voices you can pull out of your mouth, without any particular voice in mind. You are taking inventory of what the possibilities are—what voices lie hidden in the bushes, the nooks, and the crannies. Voice gathering requires a lot of uncensored play, like singing in the shower. (Many voice actors keep a small, digital recorder on them at all times—except, maybe, when they're in the shower singing—to help them recall special voices they hear or voices that jump out of them unexpectedly.)

For this playful "gathering," you almost always have to be alone, because you will sound monumentally goofy, making all manner of vocal sounds in order to plum the depths of vocal possibilities. How do you do this? Through vocal adjustments called "Pitch, Placement, Position, and Push" (see page 199). Read on.

OF BIMBOS AND BUFFOONS: VOCAL ARCHETYPES ⊙78

The human voice has astonishing range—the ability to swoop, in an instant, from highs to lows, from a whisper to a wail. Quite aside from words, there is a huge amount of information packed into the mere *sound* of a voice. We subconsciously scour and data mine the sound of others' voices for clues about their emotions and intentions. A shrillness, a tightening, a slight hesitation, a tremor—a rise in pitch here, a slight emphasis there—are all clues to a person's true character and intentions, their health, wealth, social status, and state of mind.

The good news is that we do this unconsciously. We learned it at a very early age and now don't have to think about it. It is a fundamental part of being the aware, social-climbing primates that we are.

Based on these subtle voice qualities and our communal perceptions of them, archetypal voices and characters have evolved. The meddling old woman, the doddering old man, the bimbo, the buffoon, the scary monster—these are all examples of archetypes that tiptoe through nearly every culture. Vocal characters are a cultural shorthand that communicates instantly, whether we are crouching around a fire telling stories; taking in theater, film, sitcoms, or sermons; or just cracking an off-color joke.

THE SOUND OF YOUR VOICE

Have you ever heard yourself on a tape recorder and asked, "Do I really sound like that?" Well . . . yes. If you are surprised by the sound of your voice, you're not alone. Most people spend very little time listening to their own voices. To begin with, we normally hear our own voice in a special way: at very close range—directly from our mouth, no more than six inches away from our ears. (Few

Impersonations vs. Impressions

An *impersonation* occurs when an actor re-creates the voice and mannerisms of another individual, for dramatic effect and sometimes comedy. An impersonation is a portrait of someone—an actor pretending to *be* that person. Examples include Hal Holbrook seemingly inhabiting the frame of Mark Twain, Frank Gorshin recreating comedian George Burns, Gwyneth Paltrow bringing poet Sylvia Plath to life in the film *Sylvia*, and Nicole Kidman—rubber nose and all—portraying writer Virginia Woolf in *The Hours*.

An *impression* is usually not a realistic portrait. It is a sketch or cartoon, usually for comedy. Impressions tend to involve a more personal viewpoint of the actor, as he or she imitates the person, often exaggerating physical characteristics, mannerisms, and speech for comedic effect. Television shows like *Saturday Night Live* use impressions of well-known public figures for comedy and satire.

Creating impressions, impersonations, and accents requires a very specific skill set. Most impersonators and impressionists, however, begin by creating characters based on voice and manner studies.

people, other than family and lovers, ever speak that close to you.) We also hear our voice as it resonates through the bones in our head, which tends to make us perceive it as deeper than it is. Second, our voice sounds different to us because psychologically we *want* it to sound a particular way. When we are presented with hard evidence that our voice sounds different than we expect— usually higher and much less robust than we imagine—many of us get uncomfortable and say, "Oh, turn that thing off!"

Try this experiment. First, say something—the alphabet, for instance—and listen to your voice. Now, take two hardcover books and put the spine of the books against either side of your head, just in front of your ears. Immediately repeat what you just said, and listen to the difference. For most people the difference is dramatic. Your voice probably sounds higher and breathier than you thought. The reason this happens is that the books block the path of your voice as it travels that small distance from your mouth to your ears. By reflecting your voice around the room, the books force you to hear your voice more in the manner that others hear it.

Women, Men, and Voices

In Western culture, women tend to invest their voices with much more animation than men—in fact, they use decidedly different voices for different tasks. There are many reasons for this, but chief among them, according to psychologists, is that women in this society play many more roles than men do.

Most men speak within a range of three to four notes, rarely venturing higher or lower. They use the same voice at work as they do at home, except, perhaps, in moments of intimacy with family or when shouting at the TV screen over a punt return. Combine this with men's tendency to conceal their emotions, and you end up with relatively expressionless, monotone voices.

Women's voices, on the other hand, change constantly to reflect their constantly changing roles—mother, social organizer, worker, coquette ... the list goes on. Anecdotally: Let's say all hell breaks loose in the house. The mother is shouting at the kids, "Get the dog off the sofa!" And then the phone rings. Suddenly the mother answers with a calm, sweet voice, "Hellooooo?" Or, in a café, over coffee, a woman—speaking deeply, under her breath, from the side of her mouth about work problems, looks up to the passing waiter and coos in an impossibly high and girlish voice, "May I have another cup of coffee, ple-eeeeease?" The changeup is awe inspiring.

TAKING CARE OF YOUR VOICE

Your voice is probably one of the best indicators of good health or health problems. Almost everything shows up, one way or another, in your voice: oncoming colds, shaky emotional states, too much partying. What's good for your general health—sleep, a balanced diet, lots of water, etc.—is good for your voice, and vice versa. Here are several specific things you can do to take care of your voice:

- **Don't scream and shout at ballgames, parties, and the like.** You can whistle, clap, and stomp to your heart's content, but excessive yelling truly hurts your voice. If you ever come home hoarse from an event or party, you've overdone it. (Doing this repeatedly can actually put little blisters, calluses, and scar tissue on the edges of your vocal folds, giving you a permanently raspy "smoker's" voice—considered sexy in some circles, but brutal for actors and voice professionals.)

- **Never, ever use any lozenges or sprays—they superficially deaden the feeling in your throat.** Candies and cough drops are fine, but anything that artificially hides your throat's sensitivity can allow you

Awesome Party Tip #38

"Talk under the din." If you are at a loud party and find yourself shouting louder and louder just to talk to people, begin speaking "under the noise." What is happening is that the voices in the room are competing in the same frequency range—so people raise their volume and their pitch when they feel they can't be heard. They shout in high voices. All you have to do is not compete. Talk in a quieter, deeper voice, and you will be heard easily. Try it. You will be shocked at how easy it is to talk under the din.

to further injure your voice—without even feeling it. (Throat pain is nature's way of saying "Shut up, already!") Feeling a scratchiness in your voice and

Creature Voices: Monsters, Aliens, and Animals

To transform your voice into that of a monster, an alien creature, or an animal, you might begin with a voice that you discover yourself, and then create your own creature from that voice. Or start the other way around, with a creature whose voice you have never heard. It is best to begin with at least a mental picture of the creature. A drawing, sketch, model or puppet is even better.

The physical characteristics of the creature—its size and shape, and particularly its mouth—will strongly affect your choice of voice. Look at its skin covering: Is it reptilian with scales or mammal-like with fur? It may have skin that is moist or gooey or made of metal, or maybe it has a brittle exoskeleton, like an insect. These factors affect the voice, but the single most important factor is this: Do you want others to like the creature or not?

The personality of the creature determines so much about the voice. The big, brutal monster will usually have a deep, sinister voice to match. But a big, nice monster will probably have some soft qualities in his voice. As a rule, fast-talking creatures are perceived as more intelligent, while slower talkers seem slower witted. (See Stoopid and Slo, page 212.) But all these rules are made to be broken. A voice works because it makes a creature come alive.

throat is usually a sign that something is out of balance. Herbal teas and warm liquids are fine, but good, clean tap water is the very best for hydration.

- **Gargle this: No product ever created has the natural, curative properties of warm salt water.** Mix a little sea salt with warm tap water so that it tastes only about as salty as ocean water. Gargle, and even sniff this through your nose from the palm of your hand, spitting it out through your mouth. This is the way noses and throats have been maintained around the world for thousands of years.

If you are prone to sinus and throat conditions, you might try finding a "neti cup" or "neti pot," an ancient little gravy-boat-of-a-cup that helps you do this easily. No joke. It has changed lives.

Hamlet and Gollum

Actors take widely different paths in their discovery of characters within themselves. Sir Laurence Olivier, one of the great British actors of the twentieth century, said that he found characters "by a nose." He would apply appropriate makeup to change his nose, particularly for his theatrical Shakespearian roles, and then let the nose inform him—guide him to his voice and the discovery of the inner character.

Andy Serkis, another British actor, who plays the wide-eyed, schizophrenic Gollum/Smeagol in *The Lord of the Rings* trilogy, says his house cat guided him to the voice of Gollum. One day he noticed the sound it made when throwing up a hair ball—a throaty, breathy, raspy gag from far back in the throat. Luckily, he happened upon this idea for the voice of Gollum just before an audition with the director, Peter Jackson. Try this: Imagine coughing up a fur ball, create the sound far back in your throat, and say "... my precious ..." and you've got it.

VOICE TECHNIQUES

Characters can be inspired and created in many ways (see "Hamlet and Gollum"). But now we're talking techniques. Instead of teaching a few specific character archetypes by imitation or acting methods, here are a few techniques and vocal effects to apply to your own voice, so that you can find your own old man or baby or creature voices within.

(To butcher an ancient Chinese proverb, this book does not simply give you a fish, it teaches you *how* to fish—or, failing that, at least teaches you how to do a good fish impression, page 83.)

Your voice, after some pushing and prodding, will become your own guide to characters.

When you hear something that has possibilities for the character you want to create, practice a few lines. Play with it, push it—be fearless. Then when it sounds right, lock it down. You can do this by recording it or, as many professional voice-over people do, practice a specific catchphrase over and over—a phrase that seems to embody the character and voice. (See Author's Note, page 202.)

PITCH, PLACEMENT, POSITION, AND PUSH ⊙78

So how do you uncover or discover a new voice? By Pitch, Placement, Position, and Push. These are the main variables, the adjustments that you balance and weigh, combine and stir, to shape new voices.

Pitch

Pitch is how high or low a character's voice range will be. There are rules of thumb, but great voices sometimes

199

flout the rules and thereby become truly original (see "Hamlet and Gollum" and "He Ain't Heavy," page 198 and below). The rule of thumb is obvious: Voice size tends to correspond with creature size. The smaller the character, the "smaller" and higher the voice; the bigger the character or creature, the deeper the voice. (See "Creature Voices: Monsters, Aliens, and Animals," page 197.)

Other than simply raising and lowering your voice, you can increase the pitch of a character by speaking in falsetto. The voice of Mickey Mouse is a classic falsetto voice, originally performed by Walt Disney himself. (See the Falsetto, page 23).

For especially low voices, try relaxing your throat and exhaling deeply from the diaphragm (see Diaphragm, page 3) or create the voice while *inhaling* (see Back Talk, page 203). This will give you a Darth Vader deep voice, good for alien creatures. You may try adding other special pitch effects such as voice breaks or yodels (see Yodeling, page 14).

Placement

Placement is *where* you center the voice—where the voice *feels* like it's coming from (chest, upper or lower throat, nose, back or front of mouth). Try a voice placed normally in the throat. Take any phrase, like "Hello, how are you?" and repeat it in varying positions. Try opening up the throat and pushing the sound

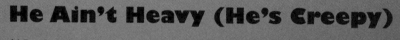

He Ain't Heavy (He's Creepy)

"**H**eavies" in film (those evil, menacing roles) tend to have deep voices to match, but frightening exceptions abound, from Tony Perkins in *Psycho* to Jack Nicholson in *The Shining*. High, light voices can reflect a deeply disturbing sense of repressed rage, tinged with psychotic volatility—think Vincent Price or Roddy McDowall, or Strother Martin as the jail warden in *Cool Hand Luke*.

farther down into the chest. For a more nasal SpongeBob cartoon sound, try arching the tongue up in the back of the mouth to kick the voice into the nose and "squeeze" the voice upward—"Hello, how are you!" Move it very far forward in the front of the mouth for a "thinner," more childlike sound.

Position

Position is shorthand for how the teeth, tongue, mouth, jaws, and lips are set to shape the sound. Various mouth positions add color and eccentricity to any voice. You might try jutting the jaw forward, thickening the tongue, feigning a severe head cold or stopped-up nose, loosening the lips slightly or pushing them to the side. Try puffing out the cheeks on certain words (Roger Rabbit's "P-p-p-p-lease, Eddie") or try various speech "impediments" such as a front tongue-lisp (Daffy Duck's "thufferin' thuckotash"), or a lateral tongue-lisp (where air escapes around the sides of the tongue; see the box titled "Ice Age, Sid" below). Cartoon voices tend to be the most exaggerated and highest energy. Finding such extremes and then gently dialing back the effect is an excellent way to find more subtle voices.

Ice Age, Sid

Often full, highly successful voices are inspired by one small voice detail. In the movie *Ice Age*, John Leguizamo created the voice of Sid the Sloth with a wicked lateral lisp. Apparently, he tried dozens of voices and nothing seemed to work, until, after watching hours of Discovery Channel sloth footage, he heard the narrator say that sloths store food in their cheeks. He immediately began riffing on the notion of cheek placement and positioning, and suddenly the voice of Sid emerged—in its full, lateral-lisp glory.

Push

Push is the word used to describe breathing and energy. Once you have some idea of the pitch, placement, and position of a voice, breathing becomes key. Breathing affects both speed and energy, as well as voice quality. Voices, at any given pitch, can range from slow and whispered to loud and fast, simply by changing how quickly and forcefully you push the voice. You can add a heavy or light raspiness to the voice to soften or age it. Or add depth, resonance, and authority to it by breathing deeply, opening the throat, and pushing deeply from the diaphragm. (See Breathing, page 5.)

The Character Catchphrase (Author's Note)

Professional actors have to switch between different voices all the time. But each individual character must have rock-solid consistency over time. A technique for recalling and locking in a voice is to create a "catchphrase" for that character. This phrase, repeated just before reading actual lines, will pull the actor back into the correct voice placement for the character.

For instance, on the Nickelodeon and Disney/ABC series *Doug*, I perform the voices of Doug's best friend, Skeeter; Doug's next door neighbor, Mr. Dink; and Ned, one of Roger's gang, among others. As I switched back and forth among characters in recording sessions, especially early in the series, I would occasionally have to reestablish a character in my head. For Skeeter, I would say, "Cool, man" (pronounced "cool, ban" in his nasally adenoidal, falsetto voice). I could hear Skeeter and lock on. For Mr. Dink, I used "Hello, Douglas," my teeth hissing a bit on my bottom lip. For Ned, I would say "Gee, Rog, don't hurt me . . ." Each line brought the character back for me.

BACK TALK

Vocal Effects

Your voice is unique to you, unlike anyone else's voice. But you are in no way limited to that single voice you call your own. Vocal effects are simply special effects for your voice. You can apply vocal effects to dramatically shape your voice into new and completely original voices. You may layer each effect separately onto your voice or in combination with others to create a greater range of characters, from infants to eighty-year-olds, monsters to buffoons, aliens to robots. Experiment and listen to what happens. Use effects for plays, presentations, jokes, stories, and just clowning around.

First introduced in the Animal Sounds chapter, Back Talk is an excellent base for such realistic sounds as dog barks and bird squawks. But you can also use Back Talk to imagine huge, deep-throated monsters.

INSTRUCTIONS

1. Back Talk involves speaking while *inhaling.* See instructions for the Inhaled Fry, page 27.
2. Practice. This inhaled Back Talk voice sounds very different from your normal voice, and it

may be difficult to speak words clearly at first, but it forms a strong, inhuman sound for larger creatures, aliens, and scary monsters.

USES

It is great for ghost stories and the groaning of deep space atmospherics. Use it for guttural, sinister growls, perhaps with a few long, low, menacing words, like "get . . . out . . ."

Try cupping your hands over your mouth and nose to change the sound.

For other kinds of creatures, try two other voice effects: the deep-throated Tuvan Voice (page 206) for large creatures and the Vent Voice (page 208) for smaller ones.

AGING THE VOICE

As people age, their voices age. Vocal folds become less flexible and muscles become weaker, and so voices become raspier, thinner, and more whispery. Singers and actors, as members of their local vocal gyms, however, keep their voices sounding young with traditional exercise and a healthy diet. And so can you. But in the meantime, if you just want to age your voice temporarily, read on.

INSTRUCTIONS

1. Take in a breath of air and hold your breath. Notice that, to hold your breath, you close off something in your throat—that something is actually your False Vocal Folds (see page 4). (For example, you close off your lungs when you pick up something heavy or exert yourself. When you say the sounds "uhh-uhh," you can feel your false vocal folds, especially between the sounds. You are shutting the false vocal folds in your throat, pushing air against them, until it pushes through suddenly and you vocalize the "uh" sounds.)

2. Increase air pressure, letting air seep out, until you can talk through these closed vocal folds in a whispery, raspy voice. (What you are actually doing is speaking, more or less normally, with your vocal folds, but closing your false vocal folds above them to get the raspy quality.) If no phrase comes to mind to practice with, say, "Let me tell you something, Mabel. Don't ever try to shave a cat . . ." Repeat it a few times with the rasp. Your voice will sound well-aged. For an old woman's voice, men should speak in a Falsetto (page 23) and do the same as above.

3. Practice speaking with different degrees of raspiness by tightening and loosening your upper throat. Raise your pitch and you will sound much older. Try adding a bit of quaver.

USES

For a scary witch voice, add more nasality to your raspy old woman, and force the sound out more strongly—the stronger the voice, the scarier the witch. Of course, adding a soaring, cackle-laugh helps, too.

Raspiness is a great quality to add to voices to show age, character, or the effects of too much high-life. Adding this raspiness to a youthful voice gives the character just a hint of burnout from too much partying. Adding it to a friendly, enthusiastic voice will conjure the voice of a friendly bartender in a Western movie. Because there is not a lot of volume with

these voices, they are especially convincing when amplified over a telephone or microphone.

THE TUVAN VOICE

You need a waiver from your lawyer before you try this. It is an extremely odd sensation, and if you overdo it, it can cause you to cough for a moment. Stop immediately if you feel any throat discomfort. (See "Taking Care of Your Voice," page 196.)

INSTRUCTIONS

1. Listen to the demo on the CD. You can actually speak in a shockingly deep, gravelly voice by speaking, not with your vocal folds as normal, but solely with your false vocal folds (page 4).

2. Follow the first two steps for Aging the Voice (page 204), but as you speak, let air seep out and relax your throat as if you are saying or singing the lowest note you can.

3. Experiment very gently. You will soon hear a deep buzzing that may be difficult to control. This buzzing is one of the tones used by

206

Tuvan Throat-Singing

Throat-singing is a vocal technique found in several cultures, particularly in northern Asia. Its haunting, ethereal, drone-like quality is produced by singers who produce two or more distinct tones at the same time. They do this by manipulating harmonics of the throat and vocal folds, often by producing a deep buzzing of the false vocal folds.

Known as overtone singing, biphonic singing, or harmonic singing, throat singing is practiced by groups of Tibetan monks, herdsmen of Mongolia, and, surely most notably, by many residents of Tuva, in a part of extreme southern Siberia in Russia. The acoustics of throat-singing are very complex and still not entirely understood.

Buddhist monks for harmonic throat singing. Very little breath is needed. You do not need to push hard. These little flaps of skin—your false vocal folds—are probably unaccustomed to vibrating, unless, of course, you are a Mongolian herdsman.

You will, most likely, feel a new sensation, a sensation that may make you cough if you force too much air. *Do not continue* if you feel discomfort. You can speak in this voice, although very softly. This deep, gravelly voice can be used for scary aliens, monsters, and animal voices.

Additionally, it is quite possible, simultaneously with this deep buzzing of the false vocal folds, to speak or sing another tone with your normal vocal folds. It creates a fascinating, deep, rich drone effect.

THE VENT VOICE

Ventriloquism, or what professionals call "vent," works not because the ventriloquist "throws his voice," but because he or she misdirects the audience, much like a magician. Some object, usually a hand, a puppet, or a dummy, moves in time with the ventriloquist's words. The ventriloquist simultaneously speaks without apparent mouth movement. The audience hears the voice and sees the dummy's lips move, and the magic happens: The dummy appears to be alive and speaking. (Ventriloquists put their teeth lightly on their bottom lip so their mouth appears relaxed and more or less closed,

and they substitute "v's" and "f's" for lip-moving sounds like "b's" and "p's." So "put the ball back" comes out a bit like "fut the vall vack.")

The most effective ventriloquists also do something else: They mute their voice a bit. It actually sounds like it is coming from someplace other than their mouth, and in some ways, it is. Much less of it comes out the mouth, and more of it comes out the nose and resonates from the throat. Here is how you can try this ventriloquist effect.

INSTRUCTIONS

1. Make a comfortable "aaaah" sound.

2. Now, as you say "aaaah," imagine that you are gargling. Tilt your head back, pull the very back of your tongue as far back in your throat as you can, and arch it up so that it nearly closes off your mouth from your throat. Your "aaaah" should nearly be squeezed off and take on a nasal quality. (Your tongue and throat are in a position similar to gargling or gagging.)

3. Holding this position, now speak. Your voice should sound strangely muted. Play with this long enough to get comfortable. Sing "Bah, Bah, Black Sheep" or "London Bridge." (Songs are good because you can feel and experiment with the elongated vowel tones as they resonate in your nose.)

4. Your voice should sound almost as if it is coming out of your throat or nose—not your mouth. The more the voice shifts away from your mouth, the more difficult it is to articulate into words. Balance the muting effect with word articulation, until you mute your voice but can hear the words clearly. (It helps to overarticulate each word.)

5. You are now doing the Ventriloquist Voice. (For other ventriloquist effects, see also the Stealth Bark, page 51, and the Phone Voice, page 163). This is a great voice to use for magical dwarfs and other little creatures, and cartoon beings of all sorts.

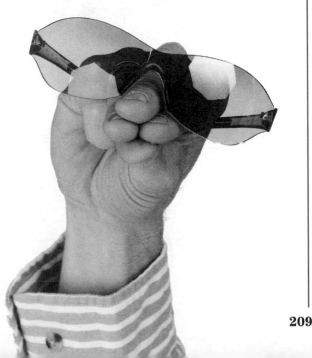

THE BABY VOICE

Creating the voices of babies, small animals, and cute aliens can be enhanced with the Vent Voice (page 208). What all those beings have in common, besides their cuteness, is a very small larynx. Now you can shrink the size of your vocal resonance to snuggle up close to that cuteness.

INSTRUCTIONS

1. Follow the steps for the Vent Voice (page 208).
2. Instead of muting your regular voice, take your voice into a high falsetto (page 23) and mute it by pulling it far back into your throat.

Practice a bit to catch the cuteness of a baby. Try saying *baby* and *pretty puppy*, kicking the voice high in pitch and up into your nasal mask. Sing, laugh, and cry.

USES

What you have done is shrink the size of your upper throat so that it resonates much like that of any small creature. This voice, along with many variations of it that you can find, can be used for fantasy elves, gremlins, fairies, and dwarves, along with cute, furry cartoon and puppet animals.

Also, let us not forget that this cute voice makes an excellent voice for inanimate objects such as lamps, stuffed animals, kids' shoes (while on their feet), and beer bottles. Animate the object with your hand as you speak the Baby Voice. Pick up a child's foot and let it ring (see Cell Phone Ring, page 162) and be the voice on the other end of a quick phone call—all while the child's shoe is pressed to your ear. Watch the surprise. Or have your beer bottle say a few words to you in a bar, and watch as the fun begins . . . or your drinking privileges are revoked.

The Five Stages of a Cryin' Baby

◉ 82

A good baby cry is an excellent tool to have in your vocal kit bag. Women will respond immediately, instinctively compelled by an odd mix of compassion and panic. A distant baby crying can stop a speech or quiet a room quicker than a fire alarm.

There are five basic stages of baby crying, each stage having a distinct sound, rhythm, and meaning. In each, your starting point for making the sound is the Baby Voice.

Stage 1:	Stage 2:	Stage 3:	Stage 4:	Stage 5:
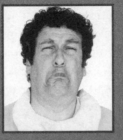	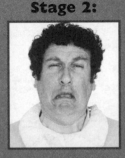		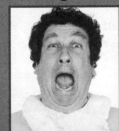	

Stage 1:

Prickly Heat

(A long, gurgling, cooing complaint—general irritation with the state of affairs)

Translation: *"Can I have a word with you? Excuse me?"*

Stage 2:

The Hiccup Cry

(An insistent, slightly rhythmic whining)

Translation: *"Hey! Yo! Little help here!"*

Stage 3:

The Jungle Motif

A loud, rhythmic car-alarm of a cry (also known as "the peacock")

Translation: *"All right, so that's the way you wanna play. Let's get the neighbors involved!"*

Stage 4:

The Big Whaaa

(A huge, soul-rippin' wail emitted with a sense of deep disdain)

Translation: *"You call yourself . . . a parent?!!"*

Stage 5:

The Grand Mawl

(A big "whaaa" that abruptly stops, as baby stops breathing altogether and turns blue. After a long moment, cry picks up where it left off)

Translation: *"I'm going down . . . and I'm taking you with me . . ."*

STOOPID 'N' SLO

A classic character from jokes, fables, and fairy tales is the dim-witted, thick-skulled anti-hero—the stoopid guy. For characters with *way* low processing speed, try the "Stoopid 'n' Slow" vocal effect.

INSTRUCTIONS

1. The Happy-Stoopid Effect: Add very slow, breathy laughter to a soft, lower voice—"heeeh, heeeh, heeeeeh."

2. Let your character choose his or her words painfully slowly and you will cause an IQ avalanche. A sort of lovable quality comes with this voice. A few "gah-huk, guh-huk" laughs and it's Stoopid on Parade.

Vocal Energy: Ordinary Joe to Over-the-Top

Voices must tap into the energy of the medium for which they are created. There is a real difference in energy between the voice of an ordinary off-the-street Joe and that of an actor in a movie. Actors are trained to add just the right amount of stylized energy into lines to add drama and life to a voice while keeping it totally believable. This is not so obvious in serious film, but you can certainly hear the added energy in commercials, sit-coms, theater, and cartoons. By way of example of the range (and not at all scientific) a real-life conversation in bed might be a 1; film a 2; television sitcoms and comedies a 3; commercials and theater a 4; and cartoons and early Jim Carrey, a face-distorting 5 or more.

When you create new voices, always remember your medium and audience—how and to whom you will be using your voice. Some voices only work in the high energy of a stage show or farce, while others work beautifully over a telephone or in quiet, microphone-amplified situations.

SLICK 'N' SMART

For every classic character that's "stoopid 'n' slow," there is the reverse—the quick-talking shyster, who is far too agile and angular in voice.

INSTRUCTIONS

1. Crispen a character's diction and make the character speak quickly, and he or she will appear to be much smarter.
2. Now throw in your best used-car-salesman sleeze and your character is ready for some wheeling and dealing.

USES

This makes a good voice for characters ranging from harmless, smart geeks to weasely, slick salespeople.

THE NEBBISH EFFECT

When you need to create a voice with a touch of sad, mildly comic, down-trodden resignation, summoning up the Nebbish Effect can help. The Nebbish himself is the beloved, hard-pressed milquetoast saying, "Yes, dear . . ." to the domineering wife. Layer a touch of the jowly Nebbish Effect on any voice and you'll get instant sympathy for your character.

INSTRUCTIONS

1. Try saying the words, "The blue blanket billows in the breeze" in a moderately high, unenthusiastic voice. Keep your cheeks very loose.

2. As you say each "b" sound, let your cheeks fill a bit with air—let them billow—and then fall naturally as you continue. Let the cheeks flop a bit, use a slightly depressed, monotone of a voice, and you become the nebbish.

USES

The result can be used for well-intentioned but hard-pressed nerds of all sorts. It can be delivered in a lifeless manner or, for interesting effect, with high energy and eagerness. The best character voices, however, are not just one-dimensional. Add the Nebbish Effect to you voice, but keep the inner fire, repressed, but glowing deep. And don't feel too sorry for the nebbish; in many stories, it is the nebbish who eventually triumphs over all.

THE ROBOT VOICE

The classic Robot Voice is certainly electronic and tends, therefore, to be flat and emotionless. The slightly unnerving, disembodied nature of the voice is the quality you want to convey. Here is how you can approximate some silicon syllables:

INSTRUCTIONS

1. In a flat monotone, say any sentence, such as "Please pass me that shot glass of oil over there."
2. As you say the sentence again, now take your pointing finger and waggle it up and down between your lips. You will hear the robotic effect. Another, more subtle way to make your voice quaver is to gently wiggle one or two fingers up and down on your Adam's apple as you speak. You will hear a more gentle vibration in the voice.

USES

You can combine this electronic modulation of the voice with a bit of the Howard Sprague effect (page 216). This will pull your voice back into your throat, making your robot voice even more convincing.

Still another way to simulate an electronic robot voice is by talking into a large drinking glass or big plastic cup. Talk slightly into the mouth of the glass and the voice that emerges has a true ring of electronica to it.

215

THE SPRAGUE EFFECT

Named in honor of Howard Sprague, a character on the old *Andy Griffith Show* (the persnickety Mayberry town clerk who lived with his mother) the Sprague Effect says, "I'm nerdy, I'm none too bright, and I don't got a clue about either."

But it's not so much about the character as it is about the hollow, nasal sound.

INSTRUCTIONS

1. First, listen to the CD, because the voice is easier to hear than describe. It is much like a gentler version of the Vent Voice (page 208).

2. Make a comfortable, mid-voiced "aaaah."

3. Arch the back of your tongue as you say "aaah," giving it a strange, nerdlike nasal quality. Now speak in this voice. Bingo. The Howard Sprague effect.

USES

Add the Sprague Effect to almost any voice and come up with entirely new ones. Try doing an impression (see page 194) of someone you know and color it with the Sprague Effect.

You can apply the Sprague Effect ever-so-slightly or push it far into the realm of Warner Brother's cartoon character Marvin the Martian.

Tongue arched in back places the voice more in the nose.

Trombone Garble

⦿ 90

"Trombone garble" is how it was officially catalogued in the original card files of Warner Brothers' cartoon sound-effects library. It's the sound of a cartoon whose legs and body have outrun its neck and head—which hover momentarily in the air, before being snatched off-camera to catch up with its scampering feet. It's the sound of a hunter's hand throttling a duck's neck—a cartoon getting clothes-lined. A classic sound effect. How was it made?

Actually, it was Mel Blanc saying "ah-ee, ah-ee, ah-ee" rapidly into the mouthpiece of a trombone with a touch of staccato throat jitter (a sort of machine-gun effect). Try it. If you don't have a trombone (and just think of the fun you're missing), try a wrapping-paper or toilet-paper tube.

MEEP! MEEP!

"I Tawt I Taw a Puddy Tat . . ."

Cartoon voices are thoroughly infectious and captivating. They are some of the first voices that many of us notice and try to imitate. Cartoon voices—from Tweety Bird to SpongeBob—owe their existence to one man.

From the late 1930s, Mel Blanc created the voices of nearly every cartoon character in the Warner Brothers cartoon stable: Porky Pig, Bugs Bunny, Daffy Duck, Sylvester the Cat, Tweety Bird, Yosemite Sam, Road Runner, and the Tasmanian Devil. He infused each character with an eccentric energy. Many sported tough Brooklyn accents, and, nearly always, flamboyant speech impediments ("Thufferin' Thuckatash!"). This tradition of high-energy characters, often laced with unusual lisps and diction, is very much with us today.

What many don't know is that Mel Blanc, along with Disney's Jimmy McDonald, invented sound-effect design for cartoons as well. A lot of the crazy effects that are now standard fare—boings, twangs, sputters, swooshes, and ricochets—were originally created by Mel Blanc using his mouth sounds with various cups, tubes, and musical instruments. It's just part of the lingering legacy of Mel Blanc's genius.

We all know the sound of the Road Runner's classic "Beep! Beep!" If you want to re-create this sound, here's how:

INSTRUCTIONS

1. First, in a mid- to high-range, nasal voice, say "Beep, beep." Say it a few times, pushing sharply and forcefully from your diaphragm (see page 3). Push the sound up high into the space behind your nose.

2. Keeping the sound nasally, say "Meep, meep." The "m" sound kicks it clearly into the nose. Try humming an "mmm," just as you say "meep." Say "Meep! Meep!" sharply and quickly, and you'll hear the familiar Road Runner honk. Meep! Meep!

CHAPTER 10

SOUND STORIES

A story: beginning, middle, end. Boom. That's it. Simple. We're humans. We sing, rap, rhyme. It's what we do. We gossip, we joke, we talk about our trips, our teeth, our taxes—everything, endlessly. Stories. Our stories *are* who we are. Human history, in every culture—anywhere, anytime— is the sum of all its stories. Think about it. Even religious wars are fights over stories. We can't *not* tell a story. Until recently, anthropologists defined *Homo sapiens* as the "toolmaking animals." But we now know better.

Animals from ants to apes make and use tools, too. Storytelling is the only thing that truly distinguishes us from all other animals on earth. It is what we do. We throw cocktail parties to share stories. We make television and movies to tell stories. We watch sports to see stories unfold. (That's why everybody hates a tie game—because the story has no ending.) In a Darwinian sense, we have survived as a species, climbing to the very tip of the evolutionary pile by binding our cultures together and passing on our accumulated wisdom through stories.

THE OVER (AND UNDER) VIEW

This book, in its broadest terms, is a guide, an exploration, and a celebration of the human voice. Nowhere are the many colors and facets of the voice so obviously displayed, as in the service of a good story.

Sound stories represent the culmination of the preceding chapters, which are designed to be a sort of vocal yoga—they open up the ear and limber up the voice. Here are five very different stories meant to be told aloud—to be read to children at bedtime, told at dinner, performed around a fire, or shared in classrooms, picnics, and family gatherings. Play with them (listening to the CD will help), keeping what works for you and discarding what feels wrong. You can read the story aloud from the book, perform it as a script, or, best of all, completely retell the story in your own words. The most important thing is that it becomes yours—you must *own* the story.

THE TAR BABY

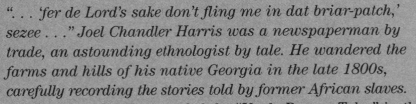

"... 'fer de Lord's sake don't fling me in dat briar-patch,' sezee ..." Joel Chandler Harris was a newspaperman by trade, an astounding ethnologist by tale. He wandered the farms and hills of his native Georgia in the late 1800s, carefully recording the stories told by former African slaves.

Harris faithfully recorded the "Uncle Remus Tales" in the African-American dialect prominent in the area at the time, making his stories an unparalleled treasure trove for both folklorists and linguists around the world. The originals make for difficult reading today and have most often been translated with a tin ear for the original oral tradition they represent, as well as a hypersensitivity to political correctness.

The characterization of the fictional narrator, Uncle Remus, as a "happy former slave" lingers as a symbol of the whitewashing of American history. But setting aside issues involving the narrator, most linguists and folklorists of all races agree: The rhythms, messages, sounds, and sensibilities are all there, making these stories the best transcriptions available of the African-American folktale of the "trickster rabbit."

One day, after Brer Rabbit had fooled Brer Fox one too many times, Brer Fox decided he was gon get even. He went to work and got himself some tar, and he mixed it up with turpentine [GOOEY STIRRING], and fixed up a contraption that he called a Tar Baby. And he took that Tar Baby and sat her on the side of the big road [THUMP], and he lay off in the bushes to see what the news was gon be. And he didn't have to wait long, neither, 'cause, by-and-by, here comes ol' Brer Rabbit [QUICK FOOTSTEPS/DISTANT, LIGHT NONSENSE SINGING] pacin' down the road—lippity-clippity, lippity-clippity—just as sassy as a jay-bird.

Brer Fox, he lay low.

Brer Rabbit comes prancin' along 'til he sees the Tar Baby, and he **[BREATHY LITTLE WHOOP]** fetched up on his hind legs like he was surprised. The Tar Baby? She just sat there, she did.

And Brer Fox, he lay low.

[HIGH VOICE] "Mornin'!" says Brer Rabbit, says he. "Nice weather this mornin'. . ." says he.

Tar Baby ain't sayin' nothin'. And Brer Fox, he lay low.

"How're yo' complaints holdin' today?" says Brer Rabbit, says he.

Brer Fox, he winked his eye slow, and he lay low. And the Tar Baby? She ain't sayin' nothin'.

"How're you comin' on then? Are you deaf?" says Brer Rabbit, says he. "'Cause if you are, I can holler louder," says he.

Tar Baby stay still. And Brer Fox, he lay low.

Author's Note

This story of Brer Rabbit was my very favorite growing up. It's a classic, told and beloved all over the South. It was told to me by African-Americans in their strong, rolling-hills, middle-Georgia dialect, the music of which is still with me. To this day it strikes me as a particularly brilliant piece of storytelling—cinematic in its imagery, action, rhythmic cutting and repetition, like "Brer Fox, he lay low . . ."

"Brer," by the way, is short for "brother" and is pronounced as if saying "brother," except that the "th" sound in the middle is dropped—more like "Br-uh." Sounds, such as Brer Rabbit's "blip" as he first hits the Tar Baby and his "lippity-clippity" (his skipping down the road), were written into the original published work in 1880. When I heard the stories in Georgia in the 1950s, the sounds were made with mouth sounds and chest and hand claps—in the same way I imagine they were made when Joel Chandler Harris first heard the story, in the same area, three generations before.

"You know what? You are stuck up. That's what you are," says Brer Rabbit, says he. "And I'm gon cure you. That's what I'm gon do," says he.

Tar Baby sat still.

And Brer Fox . . . he lay low.

Brer Rabbit keep on askin' him, and the Tar Baby, she keep on sayin' nothing, 'til presently, Brer Rabbit draws back with his fist, he does, and—blip **["BLIIIP" OR HAND CLAP]**—he hit her up side her head.

Now, right there's where he broke his molasses jug. His fist stuck, and he couldn't pull loose. **[LITTLE STRUGGLE/ SUCTION SOUND]** The tar held him.

But the Tar Baby, she stay still . . . And Brer Fox, he lay low.

"Turn me loose, before I kick the natural stuffin' outta you," says Brer Rabbit, says he. But the Tar Baby, she ain't sayin' nothin'. She just held on. **[STRUGGLE/SUCTION SOUND]** And then ol' Brer Rabbit lost the use of his feet **[BHOOMP, BHOOMP]** in the exact same way.

Brer Fox, he lay low.

Then, Brer Rabbit squalled out that if the Tar Baby didn't turn him loose, he's gon' butt her sideways. And then he butted. **[BHOOMP]** And his head got stuck.

A little piece of time went by. Then ol' Brer Fox **[LOW, CASUAL HUMMING],** he kind of sauntered forth, lookin' just as innocent as one of yo' mama's mockinbirds.

[LOW VOICE] "Howdy, Brer Rabbit," says Brer Fox, says he. "You lookin' sorta 'stuck up' this mornin'," says he. **[LAUGHTER]** And then he rolled on the ground and laughed and laughed 'til he couldn't laugh no more.

"Looks like I got you this time, Brer Rabbit," says ol' Brer Fox. "Maybe I don't, but I expect I do. You've been running 'round here, sassin' after me a mightly long time.

"Yeah, you're always somewhere where you've got no business. Who asked you to strike up an acquaintance with this here Tar Baby? Huh? And who stuck you up, there, where you are? Nobody in the whole, wide world, but you. Well, there you are and there you'll stay until I fix up a brush pile and fire her up, 'cause, today, I'm gon' barbecue you, for sure," says Brer Fox, says he.

Then, Brer Rabbit started talking mighty fast and humble.

"I don't care what you do with me, Brer Fox," says he, "Just as long as you don't throw me in that briar patch. Roast me, Brer Fox," says he, "but DON'T fling me in that briar patch," says he.

Brer Fox thought for a moment. "Well, it's so much trouble to kindle a fire," says he, "that I expect I'll have to hang you," says he.

"You hang me. You hang me just as high as you please, Brer Fox," says Brer Rabbit, says he, "but for Lord's sake, don't fling me in that briar patch."

"I ain't got no string," says Brer Fox, says he, "and now I expect I'll have to drown you," says he.

"Oh, drown me just as deep as you please, Brer Fox," says Brer Rabbit, says he, "but don't fling me in that briar patch," says he.

"There ain't no water near here," says Brer Fox, says he, "so I expect I'll have to skin you," says he.

"That's all right, Brer Fox. Skin me," says Brer Rabbit. "Snatch out my eye-balls, tear out my ears by the roots, and cut off my legs," says he, "but please, Brer Fox, DON'T fling me in that briar patch," says he.

Now, Brer Fox wants to hurt Brer Rabbit as bad as he can, so . . . [BREATHY WHOP] he caught him by his hind legs and [WHISHHHHH] slung him right in the middle of that briar patch. [KUUSHH]

There was considerable flutter where Brer Rabbit struck the bushes [LITTLE SCREAMS AND YELLS], and Brer Fox sort of hung around to see what was gon' happen. By and by, he heard someone call him [HIGH, DISTANT "HEY!" IN FALSETTO]. And way up on the hill, he sees Brer Rabbit sittin', cross-legged on a chestnut log, combing the tar out of his hair with a wood chip.

Then Brer Fox knew he'd been swapped-short, pretty bad. And Brer Rabbit was pleased to fling some sass back at him, and he hollered out: "Bred and born in a briar patch, Brer Fox—bred and born in a briar patch!" And with that, he skipped out just as lively as a cricket in the wood fire.

Originally collected and written by Joel Chandler Harris in his book Uncle Remus: His Songs and His Sayings, *1881, illustrated by Frederick S. Church and J.H. Moser, New York, D. Appleton & Company. Retold/translated from original dialect version by Fred Newman.*

225

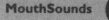

THE NEW PRESIDENT

Jokes are mini stories with a big punch at the end. They're the best examples of how most stories used to be told—with vocal animation. They are dense, topical, pointed, and they spread like epidemics.

A new country emerged on a remote island in the Pacific and the newly elected president of the country had come to the United Nations to give a speech. He was a striking chieftain, very tall and exotic in his ceremonial dress. No one knew anything about the new country or its people.

A hotshot reporter was the first to interview the new chief, and asked him **[CRISP, NASAL, REPORTER VOICE]**, "Excuse me, sir. May I ask you a couple of questions?"

The chief turned to him quite regally, smiled and said **[PINCHED, ELECTRONIC-SOUNDING]** "Bleeee . . . whiiuuu . . . crackle . . . dip . . . dip . . . dip." He pinched his nose and said, "Yes, certainly . . . whoo-iirrrrrr, t-t-t-t-t, snap."

"Oh . . . uh . . . great," answered the reporter. "Do you plan to align your country with the other island nations of the Pacific?"

The chief replied, "Zah-ooo, freeeeep, whoo-whooo-whoo, gorzit, haaaa," then pinching his nose, he added, "We plan to chart our own path."

The reporter blinked. "All . . . right. Well, ah, sir, may I ask a more personal question?"

"Blooooo, vap, whistle, siiii-uuuuu, bonk, dong, dip-dip . . . **[NOSE PINCHED]** . . . Why, of course."

"Where did you learn to speak such—good English?"

"Raaaa-oooo, zzzzzzzzzzz, bop, waa-waaa-waaa, ploit . . . **[NOSE PINCHED]** from short-wave radio . . . bleeeee-rao, snurrrrrr, snap."

Adapted from an old joke by Fred Newman

Sound Snippet

The little truth—that all of us are affected by the sounds around us—is appropriate. When you tell the joke, make the chieftain's voice sound as if the radio dial is spinning and the radio stations are drifting. Add mouth static and any other noises and sounds that you want. Little bits of music add to the surprise of the telling. The chief's actual words should be slow, pinched, a touch shouted, and BBC-announcer-like.

KNUCKLES THE CAT

*Stories can be gathered and collected from all over. Whether a
story is overheard in line at the grocery store and then retold over
the dinner table, or read in a book and recounted at the office
water cooler, let your first hearing of a story influence your
telling. In the case of this story, imagine that you are hearing
it on a hot, lazy summer day in Jack Fling's Cash 'n' Carry
Grocery. Jack Fling, a big barrel of a man, sits behind the cash
register. As a fan slowly circulates hot air, he leans back on
two legs of his chair, with a loaf of bread behind his head as a
pillow. His voice crackles and creaks, yaps and howls, laughs
and whispers . . .*

Jack Fling was having breakfast early one morning with his
wife Lois, when all the sudden, they heard a knock at the
door. [KNOCK. KNOCK. KNOCK.]
[WOMAN'S VOICE] "Jack, you expectin' somebody?"
[MAN'S VOICE] "Naw, I ain't, Lois."
[KNOCK. KNOCK. KNOCK. KNOCK.]
[LOIS] "Well, it's somebody . . ."
[JACK] "Well, lemme go see . . ." So Jack got up and
opened the door and looked out. He looked around but he
didn't see anybody so went back and sat down.
"Wasn't nobody there," he said.
No sooner had he sat down when . . . [KNOCK. KNOCK.]
[LOIS] "Jack, it's somebody. And I'm gon' see who it is."
Lois got up, went to the door, and opened it. She looked out
and all around, and didn't see anybody. And just as she was about
to close the door, she looked down.
[LOIS] "Oh, lookie here. It's a kitty cat. Jack, come over 'ere
and look."
[JACK] "Aw, Lois, you gotta stop feeding them strays . . ."
And Jack got up and saw it. "Oh, Lord, Lois! Close that door!

That ain't no kitty cat. That's a squint-eyed, yellow cat! Don't you know what a squint-eyed yellow cat is? It's the meanest thing in the tri-county area!"

Now, a squint-eyed, yellow cat is a huge, yellow cat, the size of a footstool. And it's pure mean. It has little-tiny, mean squinty eyes. And its teeth are like huge fangs, like tusks on a hog. And it has piano wire for whiskers. And it doesn't meow like a cat— it kind of growls mean at you, like a big wild animal. It has fingernails like knives, and they're so big, it has to tuck 'em under and walk on its knuckles, like a gorilla.

"It's a horrible thing, Lois. Good lord, close the door and don't let that thing in," Jack told her.

And then Lois said something awful: "But Jack, we've got to feed him." And that was it. It was all over. Knuckles the cat had come to stay.

Nothing was the same at the Fling house. Jack had some fine hunting dogs. But Knuckles just walked out under the trees and gave 'em an ugly look [MEAN REE-OOW, A CROSS BETWEEN A GROWL AND A MEOW], and the dogs. . . [YELPING AWAY]. Gone. Birds in the trees [BIRD CHIRPS], he just looked at 'em [MEAN REE-OOW], and . . . [FLUTTER AWAY]. Gone. Bugs, roaches [TONGUE CLICKS AWAY] crawled away from the house as fast as they could. Mosquitoes [HIGH, BUZZING WHINES], gone. Flowers wilted. Paint peeled. He cleaned out the place.

And Knuckles the cat ruled the roost. If ol' Jack or Lois wouldn't feed him, he'd just walk right through the screen door [CRASH], march across the kitchen [MEAN REE-OOW], open up the pantry, and help himself to a family-size can of tuna—and I don't mean the cheap stuff. No, I'm talking about the "Chunk White" you save for company. He'd just take out his fingernail, open up that can like a can opener [CAN OPENING], and knock back the whole can [WHUP], like a shot. And then throw the can over his back. He was MEAN.

And Knuckles liked nothin' more than riding in the front seat of their big, sea-foam green Chrysler DeSoto. He'd hear Jack crank it up [CAR CRANKING]—and it'd be purring [CAR PURRING]—and Knuckles would come a-runnin' like a horse. You could hear him comin' . . . [GALLOPING, FROM FAR AWAY TO CLOSE] and jump [REE-OWW! WHOOMP] into the front seat, right beside Jack. If Jack left the window up [CRASH], Knuckles'd jump right through it.

And Knuckles *had* to ride shotgun. No, sir—would not ride in the back. Lois had to ride back there.

Now, one day Jack saw in the papers that the circus had come to town, and he and Lois wanted to go, but they knew better than to take Knuckles. So they hatched themselves a plan. He'd get in the DeSoto real quiet-like and get Lois to ease him off down the hill, without cranking up. He'd coast around the corner, start her up, and Lois would tiptoe out the front door and join him. And off they'd go. Knuckles would be none the wiser.

So Jack eases out to the car. [QUIET CAR DOOR] Gets in and Lois starts to push him.

She's sweating and grunting [GRUNTING AND PUSHING]—"Jack, take your foot off the brake!"

"Oh, sorry," he calls back. And he eases off down the driveway [SOFT SWISH OF TIRES], around the curve. He looks around. No Knuckles. Cranks her up, real gently. [QUIET CRANK AND PURR OF ENGINE] No Knuckles. Lois gets in the front seat. [QUIET OPENING AND CLOSING OF CAR DOOR] No Knuckles. And just as they're about to take off . . . they hear distant hoofbeats. [GALLOPING FROM DISTANT TO CLOSE]

"Floor it, Jack!—He's on to us." [TIRE SQUEAL]

Too late. [TIRE SPINNING] Knuckles had hold of the back bumper. They weren't going anywhere. Lois got out of the front seat [CAR DOOR] and in to the back. [CAR DOOR] Knuckles jumped through the window [WEE-OWW!] into the front seat [WHUMP]—and gave Jack an ugly look. Jack put the car in drive, and [CAR ENGINE REV] off they went to the circus.

And before you know it, there was the circus. [CIRCUS CAL-LIOPE] There were the elephants [ELEPHANT TRUMPETS], and the monkeys [MONKEYS], and clowns [HONKS AND BICYCLE HORNS], and the giraffes, sticking their heads out the tops of the cages. They saw a man get shot from a cannon [EXPLOSION AND WHOOSH], and as they watched, a motor-cycle flew [MOTORCYCLE DOPPLERS BY] over their heads—from one side of the road to the other.

And then . . . Knuckles saw it first. His eyes bugged out. [AHH-OOO-GAH HORN] His whiskers sprung out like bailing wire. [BOING] His fingernails [SCH-WING] shot out like jackknives.

There it was, in a big cage—a huge, prowling, orange-striped tiger. [TIGER GROWL] Above it, in big, orange, light-up letters were the words "World's Meanest Bengal Tiger."

Knuckles leaped through the car window [REE-OWW!], and galloped into the traffic. [GALLOPING] Cars skidded this way and that. He stomped up to that cage, muscled his way through the bars, turned and faced that Bengal tiger. There they were, star-ing at each other. That Bengal tiger [DEEP GROWLING AND BREATHING] and Knuckles. [REE-OWW!] Knuckles walked [REE-OWW!], step by step, right across that cage [DEEP TIGER GROWL], challenging that tiger. And everything stopped. Clowns stopped [BICYCLE HORN CUT SHORT]. People stopped. [SUR-PRISED "LOOK!"] Traffic stopped. [TIRE SQUEALS] Even the elephants stopped. [ELEPHANT TRUMPET CUT OFF] It got so quiet you could hear the ants walking on the cotton candy.

And there they were. Nose to nose. **[TIGER GROWL AND BREATHING] [REE-OWW!]** That huge Bengal tiger and Knuckles. **[GROWL/REE-OWW!]** Seemed like the whole world was watching. Then, all of the sudden, that tiger made his move. He snapped open his mouth, inhaled, and **[GROWL TO HUGE BITE AND SWALLOW]** . . . he ate Knuckles! Whole! Nothing but his tail was sticking out of that tiger's mouth, waving.

And that big cat slowly rolled Knuckles around in his mouth, tasting him, like he was a chocolate. And apparently, that tiger didn't like what he'd selected. With a great puff of air, he spit Knuckles out **[PA-TU-IIII! SCH-BANGGG!]** so hard that he shot across the cage, into the bars, and kind of oozed down the side wall. **[SLOW OOZING-DOWN SOUND]**

But Knuckles looked totally different—and it wasn't just the tiger spit all over him. Knuckles's little squint eyes weren't so squinty anymore—they were huge, like hubcaps.

Knuckles stared and blinked a few times. And he popped up on his tippy-toes and eased out of the cage. He walked, ever so delicately, out to the street, waited for cars to pass **[CARS PASSING]**, tiptoed over to the car, quietly opened the back door **[QUIET CAR DOOR]**, got in, and politely closed the door behind him. **[CAR DOOR CLOSE]** He even applied the seatbelt. **[CHICK-CHICK]**

Lois got out of the back seat **[QUICK CAR DOOR]** and sat in the front seat. **[QUICK CAR DOOR]** And without a word, Jack Fling started off down the road. **[REV AND PURR OF ENGINE]** He and Lois looked, first at each other, and then around at Knuckles, sitting quietly in the back seat.

And Knuckles, still wide-eyed, looked back at them and went "meow." **[IN A LITTLE KITTY VOICE]**

And off Jack Fling drove. **[PURR OF ENGINE]**

By Fred Newman (based loosely on several stories he heard in Jack Fling's Cash 'n' Carry Grocery in LaGrange, GA, around 1960)

DARRELL AND BIG DOG

The Darrell and Big Dog story is one especially apt for younger storytellers and younger audiences. The sounds are optional, of course, and not too difficult. The story is modern and short, and can simply be read aloud.

Darrell and Big Dog can also be read or performed as a setup for an interactive story in a classroom. Students can make suggestions for the next day with Big Dog, such as "Darrell and Big Dog at School," and the storyteller can weave them into a totally new story.

Darrell was asleep, snoring loudly. **[SNORE, THEN SNORT AND WAKE]** He woke with a snort and sat up. He heard something that sounded like a horse galloping **[GALLOPING]** down the street. As the hoof beats grew louder, he looked out the window. It was what he'd always wanted—a dog the size of a Toyota.

Darrell ran outside. **[BIG BARKS]** The dog began to bark and dance about on his lawn.

"Aww-right!" shouted Darrell. "Come here, Big Dog!" The dog bounded over to Darrell, his great feet thundering over the lawn. **[HUGE FOOTSTEPS]** The dog was bigger than Darrell thought. He was not just huge—he was HUMONGOUS, almost the size of his dad's minivan. Darrell's glasses fogged over as the big dog panted in his face. **[BREATHY PANTING]**

"Wowie, jeeps! This is GREAT!" he said, wiping his glasses. Just then, someone strolled around the corner. It was Peech. He was the neighborhood bully who always brought Trouble with him—Trouble was his toady, creepy, sidekick friend. Peech and Trouble always picked on the neighborhood kids. Once Darrell saw Peech and Trouble give bubble gum to a dog, just so they could watch the dog chew funny.

"Hey, four-eyes!" Trouble said. Peech grabbed Darrell and was about to swing him upside down. Big Dog came up from behind and growled with a sound like a lawn mower. **[DEEP GROWL]** Trouble took one look at Big Dog and headed for home, screaming. **[YEEE-IIII]**

"Sit, Big Dog! Sit!" shouted Darrell. Big Dog did just what Darrell said. **[TWO BIG BARKS]** He sat down—right on top of Peech!

"Whoa!" yelled Peech. Darrell was surprised. But he knew what to do.

He leaned down to Peech. "Don't pick on me ever again, OK?" he said.

[MUFFLED VOICE] "OK. OK. I'll be nice . . ." answered Peech from under the dog.

Darrell was happy to finally get things straight with Peech. He ran inside the house **[FOOTSTEPS]** and flung open the door to the living room. **[DOOR BLOWN OPEN]** Big Dog galloped in behind him. **[GALLOPING]**

"Shhhhhhh . . ." his big sister shushed in a loud whisper. Darrell's sister was watching the shopping channel on TV. **[PINCHED-NOSE TV SOUND]** Darrell wanted to watch something—actually anything—else. The big dog growled low. **[LOW GROWL]**

Darrell yelled, "Sit, Big Dog. Stay!" And Big Dog did just that. **[BIG BARK]** He sat right on top of Darrell's sister—and stayed there. **[CRUNCH]**

"Oops," said Darrell.

[MUFFLED VOICE] "OK. You can watch whatever you want," said his sister from under the dog.

Darrell's father walked into the room. Big Dog growled low. **[LOW GROWL]** Before his father could even speak, Darrell called "Oh, ah. Don't sit, Big Dog! *DON'T* sit on Daddy!" The

big dog didn't sit. He *leaped* across the room, and with his huge tongue, like a warm, wet beach towel, Big Dog [HUGE SLURP] licked his father's glasses right off his face.

[MUFFLED VOICE] "Yee-iiii!" his father called. "Get this dinosaur off me!"

"Off, Big Dog! Go!" yelled Darrell. Big Dog turned, and with one, big steamy breath [HUGE SLURP] licked off Darrell's glasses, too. Then Big Dog crashed through the front door [CRASH] and galloped off down the street. [GALLOPING] He trampled the neighbor's shrubbery and left big dents in their cars. Darrell could hear traffic honking and sirens whining [DISTANT HONKS, SIRENS] in the distance . . .

"Well, I guess it's time to finish my homework," Darrell said, as he ran up the stairs to his room. "I'll bet Big Dog will be waiting for me at school tomorrow!"

His father and sister sat on the floor, motionless, staring wide-eyed at one another.

"Uh, oh . . ." his father said.

An original story by Fred Newman

HAINT-HEAD

G-g-g-ghost stories and stories of the supernatural have been favorites for thousands of years. Bathed in candlelight or the glow of a campfire, a good storyteller can breathe life into trolls, monsters, goblins, and ghosts, haints, and spirits.

[WIND BLOWING SLOWLY. SOME BIRD CHIRPS. A CROW CALL. A FROG CROAKS. CRICKETS. AN OWL.] Ever been in the woods at night and hear the birds and the crickets and the frogs suddenly get all quiet for no reason? The only thing you hear is a hiss in the wind. **[LOW HISSING WIND]** That's a haint passing through. And all the animals know it. Ever see the night suddenly go dark, the stars go out and the moon die behind a cloud? And you hear the echo of a hiss? **[HISSING WIND]** That's a haint *floating* by. **[FOOTSTEPS]** Ever been walking down a road or path and get a cold chill, a shiver—you find yourself all of the sudden walking in a patch of cold, damp, musty air? It's what a grave smells like. You're walking *through* a haint. **[LOW HISS]** And you better say a prayer, just as fast as you can.

Oh, there are haints all around. But especially here. Because right around here, there's buried treasure.

Yeah, the old folks around here know about it. A long time ago, people buried their valuables to hold on to them—pirates and robbers, and even rich folks would bury their silver and gold when war times came. During the Revolutionary War and the Civil War, all kinds of people buried their valuables here.

And, back then, they all knew how to protect their treasure. They'd find a big rock or an old tree or maybe the corner of a house to mark the spot, and they'd dig a hole, six foot deep— the height of a man—and put their treasure in. Then they'd go out and kill one of their enemies, or, if they were rich, they'd buy a fresh corpse. They'd cut off the head, and place that head,

236

upright, on top of the treasure, and bury it all. And they'd keep one little thing from that dead body—a ring, a fingernail, a tooth, or a toe, before they'd sink that headless body to the bottom of a lake or river or ocean, so it could never be found. **[QUIET BUBBLING, FADES AWAY]**

Now, the spirit of that head, totally separated from its body, would be restless, and it'd take that treasure as its own. That's what people call a Haint-head. And they're all around here. If you hear a hollow hiss in the night—almost like a whisper— **[LONG, WHISPERY SIGH]** you know there's a haint out there protecting some buried treasure.

If the owner wanted to get at the treasure, he'd take that little body part—that finger or ring—and toss it, twelve steps away

Scaring the Crap Out of People

Setting is key for a good ghost story. Save the scary stories until dark and get close enough to your audience so that you can see their eyes, and play off their expressions. A single flashlight, candle, or low, flickering light helps set the mood.

It's also important to connect the audience directly to the stories in some way—say "this story happened nearby in these woods" or "in a house just like this one." You may tell it in first person, "this happened to me . . ." or ". . . to a close friend." Many ghost stories—and sound stories in general—are told in the pres-

ent tense, so the listener experiences them with the teller. Even if the story begins in the past, you can sometimes switch to the present: "A long time ago, an old man was walking along a path, and suddenly he sees a flash of light . . ."

Most often, a soft, mysterious voice works best, with only spare use of other voices and sound effects. Let your voice float slowly and softly, so the listeners have time to use their imaginations. When you raise your voice at a critical moment, the contrast will become all the more terrifying.

from the treasure. And that Haint-head would rise up—changing shapes, into some kind of hellhound or snake or a wild, razor-back tush-hog. That Haint-head would hiss [HISSING] and hover all around that body part, leaving the treasure alone. And with the Haint-head distracted, the owner could take his treasure back again.

If anyone else, say a treasure hunter, gets close, the Haint-head will hiss. [OMINOUS HISS] At twelve steps from the treasure, the Haint-head growls an unearthly groan [INHALED GROAN] and shakes the ground [PALATE GRIND, DEEP RUMBLE]. And at six steps away, the Haint-head rises up out of the ground [WHOOSH TO SIZZLING HISS], as some kind of hellfire animal [UNEARTHLY LOW, INHALED ANIMAL GROAN], and tries to steal that trespasser's body for its own.
[WIND BLOWING SLOWLY. SOME BIRD CHIRPS. A CROW CALL. A FROG CROAKS. CRICKETS. AN OWL.]

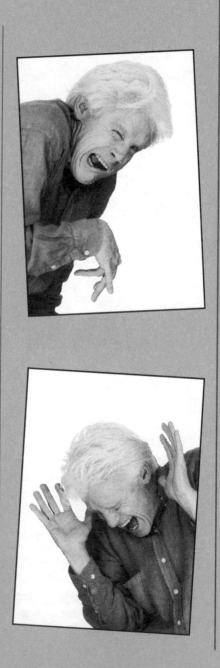

Now one day a young boy named Jimmy Jay, who lived down the road, was taking a shortcut home in the moonlight, through the woods nearby here. He'd heard the old folks' talk about Haint-heads and buried treasure, but he didn't believe in such nonsense. He's walking with a little radio, listening to music. [SLOW, DOWN-TEMPO BASS AND RHYTHM IN CUPPED HAND OR PAPER CUP FOR RADIO EFFECT]

All of the sudden, he notices the woods get all quiet. An owl hoots. [OWL WHOO-WHOO] And the stars go out. [CRICKET OR FROGS FADE TO QUIET WIND] The rhythms of the frogs and crickets disappear. It's as dark as a crow's shadow, completely quiet, except for the sound of that radio. [RADIO RHYTHM FROM ABOVE] And Jimmy hears a long hiss, echoing through the dark. [OMINOUS HISS] He takes a few more steps, [FOOT-STEPS] 1-2-3, and all the sudden, he feels the cold and clammy air, and he breathes in a foul, moldy smell. He hears another

hiss in the night. [SUBTLE HISSING] His radio is still playing. [RADIO RHYTHM, LOW] He stops and looks around. He looks up and realizes he's six steps away from the foundation stones of an old house. And the ground starts to shake [SOFT PALATE GRIND AND DEEP RUMBLE] and he hears an awful growl. [LOW, INHALED ANIMAL GROAN]

Suddenly, before he can even turn, the blue-green carcass of a dog rises up, [SIZZLING HISS] growling low. [DEEP GROWL] It has only three legs. Its ribs are sticking out of its mangy body. Its skull is half-eaten. There's blood in its eyes. Snarling and snapping [SNARLING AND GROWLING], it leaps on Jimmy, pushing him to the ground [THUD], running right over him.

The ground around him is moving, becoming liquid. [GOOEY MOVEMENT AND BUBBLING] He hears oozy bubbling. Beginning to sink, he struggles. He tries to get up, but as he does, a huge, hissing copperhead snake [SNAKE HISS] coils around his legs, rearing its great, fanged head.

Jimmy throws that radio right into that snake's mouth. And he jumps up, out of the coils, and tries to run in the muck.

But as he turns, a monstrous, glowing razorback—a tush-hog burning with hellfire—rises up from a split in the putrid earth. [BIG SCREECHING, INHALED ANIMAL CRY] Jimmy starts to run, but it's no use. That hog from hell is upon him. [HUGE PIG SQUEAL] Smoke and fire pouring from its nostrils, that great tush-hog roars. With its razor-sharp tusks and a great swipe of its head [WHIISSH], it cuts off Jimmy's head—clean. It tumbles to the ground.

Jimmy's headless body just stands there for a long moment, his head in the mud below, looking up at him, blinking, wide-eyed . . . and then, the tush-hog roars again [ROAR], even deeper and louder, shaking the trees and rocks. And that tush-hog rears up and leaps inside Jimmy's chest. [HUGE ANIMAL ROAR]

There is silence. **[OWL WHOO-WHOO]** An owl hoots. The moon breaks through. The wind blows. **[WIND QUIETLY BLOWING]** And the frogs and crickets slowly begin their night song. **[QUIET FROGS AND CRICKETS RETURN]**

Folks still talk about how, when Jimmy Jay came home that night, his parents didn't recognize him—how he never spoke again, or went to school, or said a word to any of his old friends. It was like he was a stranger. Three weeks later, he ran away from home, and it was said that he hung himself in the steeple of the church.

And some of the old folks say, when you're out in that part of the woods near the stone foundation of that old house there, and the night is real still and the moon is as dark as a crow's shadow, you can hear . . . **[SOFTLY, THE BASS AND RHYTHM OF THE RADIO DRIFTS BY]** a little radio playing in the night wind, like a whisper . . .

By Fred Newman, based on several middle-Georgia ghost tales heard growing up.

Scaring More Crap Out of People

After you tell this story, when people are in bed in the dark, you can circulate, doing just the mouth radio bass-and-rhythm very low, letting it drift in the night. People will get very creeped out.

AN AFTERWORD

. . . AND THEY LIVED NOISILY EVER AFTER

I collected mouth sounds as a kid in Georgia the way some kids collect stamps or baseball cards. Some I traded for with friends at school. Many I picked up at the feet of storytellers, larger-than-life characters who would rear back and scatter stories full of voices and sound effects, probably the way they'd heard similar stories told as far back as they could remember.

In a small Southern town, during those segregated times of the '50s and '60s, blacks and whites, surprisingly enough, came together. They came together to laugh and sip colas and swap stories—kids and old folks, the bankers beside the mill workers and field hands. The stories went right to our hearts and bound us together.

It's a scene that's been repeated around the world, across cultures, for thousands upon thousands of years—until television muscled in and took over . . .

I've spent my entire adult career, such as it is, working in sound—one way or another, in the service of storytelling. As a performer, actor, sometime musician, sound designer, and live sound-effects guy, I now dabble in just about every medium: television, film, radio, and theater. Each works because it tells stories in its own way.

The foundation of it all, I see more clearly than ever, is sound. The visuals, sometimes beautiful, sometimes astounding, sometimes disquieting, are always informational. It is the *soundtrack*, however—the voices, music, and sound effects—that carries the emotional energy and impact. (If you ever doubt that, turn off the sound during a particularly terrifying horror movie and you'll watch events with little or no alarm.)

Even as silly as I may get in this book and CD, I continue to be totally awed by the simple power of sounds and the endless possibilities of the human voice. More than any other means, it is our voice that expresses who we are. It is the sheer jazz of the voice—its energy, its purity, its playfulness—that I hope to convey. In my case, it is a jazz drawn very much from the storytellers of my youth.

NOSE WHISTLE PATTERN

For step-by-step illustrated instructions on how to assemble your paper nose whistles (one for you, one for a friend), see page 103.

Fipple Base

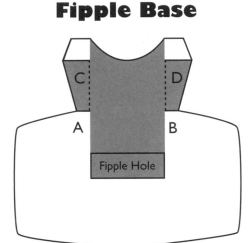

Air Guide

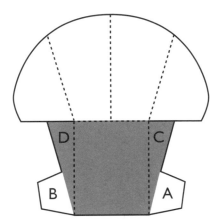

Fipple Base

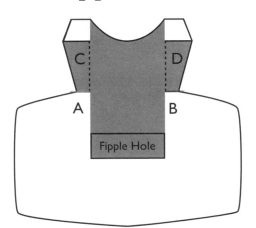

Air Guide

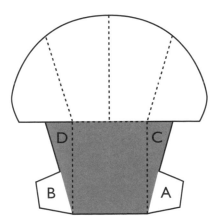